"My Heart is Overflowing…"
Psalm 45:1a NKJV

True Stories of Giving, Going and Generosity!

Living in the Overflow!

True Stories of Giving, Going and Generosity!

Mike Allard

True Stories of Giving, Going and Generosity!

Living in the Overflow!

Copyright © 2019 Mike Allard
All rights reserved.
ISBN: 978-0-578-62065-7

*Living in the Overflow
December 10, 2019
United States Copyright
Certificate of Registration*

*Printed in the United States of America
ISBN 978-0-578-62065-7*

*Special thanks to:
Zach Calderon - cover design
Leanna Cox - cover photos*

True Stories of Giving, Going and Generosity!

Thank you for helping me live in the overflow!

I want to dedicate this book to my beautiful wife Danielle. For the past forty years she has faithfully been the best wife a preacher boy could have found. I am blessed because of you!
We've definitely had our moments of triumph and tragedy, but love has won out every time. I'm glad you asked me to marry you all those years ago and I will forever love you Nellie!

True Stories of Giving, Going and Generosity!

Isaiah 12:3 NKJV
*"Therefore, with joy you will draw water from
the wells of salvation."*

What You'll Find...

From a Few of Mike's Friends...
Opening Thoughts...
<u>Chapters</u>

1. <u>Living in the Overflow</u>

The Best OVERFLOW Comes from the Lord!
"My heart is overflowing with a good theme; I recite my composition concerning the King; My Tongue *is* the pen of a ready writer."
(Psalm 45:1 NKJV)

2. <u>Just Enough or More Than Enough?</u>

"Full of Nothing!"
"Be anxious for nothing, but in everything by prayer and supplication, with thanksgiving, let your requests be made known to God;"
(Philippians 4:6 NKJV)

3. <u>Let it Flow!</u>

Be Generous with the Overflow!
"Give, and it will be given to you: good measure, pressed down, shaken together, and running over will be put into your bosom. For with the same measure that you use, it will be measured back to you."   (Luke 6:38 NKJV)

4. <u>Praying in the Overflow</u>

"If we are going to RECEIVE the OVERFLOW, we must pray in the OVERFLOW!"
"But seek first the kingdom of God and His righteousness, and all these things will be added to you." (Matthew 6:33 ESV)

5. <u>Worship in the Overflow</u>

Let WORSHIP flow from the OVERFLOW of the HOLY SPIRIT!
"Worship the Lord in the splendor of holiness;" (Psalm 96:9a ESV)

6. <u>Overload</u>

We will NEVER experience the OVERFLOW, if we Live in the OVERLOAD.

"And He said unto them, come ye yourselves apart into a desert place, and rest a while: for there were many coming and going, and they had no leisure so much as to eat." (Mark 6:31 KJV)

7. <u>Overflow Determines Direction</u>

Great FOCUS happens in the OVERFLOW of the Holy Spirit.

"Then Jesus was led up into the wilderness by the Spirit to be tempted by the devil" (Matthew 4:1 MEV)

8. <u>Splash!</u>

We can ENJOY the OVERFLOW if we let it OVERFLOW!

"On the last day of the feast, the great day, Jesus stood up and cried out, "If anyone thirsts, let him come to me and drink. [38] Whoever believes in me, as the Scripture has said, 'Out of his heart will flow rivers of living water.'" (John 7:37-38 ESV)

9. <u>Seated in the Overflow</u>

WAITING for Another WAVE of the OVERFLOW!

"Blessed *are* those who have not seen and *yet* have believed." (John 20:29b NKJV)

10.<u>What's Holding You Back?</u>

No Apologies Needed for a LIFE that OVERFLOWS!

"Then He said to them, "The harvest truly *is* great, but the laborers *are* few; therefore, pray the Lord of the harvest to send out laborers into His harvest. (Luke 10:2 NKJV)

11.<u>Creating A Tsunami of Love!</u>

Every Action Has a Reaction!

"His lord said to him, 'Well *done,* good and faithful servant; you were faithful over a few things, I will make you ruler over many things. Enter into the joy of your lord.'" (Matthew 25:21 NKJV)

In Closing:
About the Author

True Stories of Giving, Going and Generosity!

From a Few of Mike's Friends....

Mike and Danielle Allard take the Great Commission as seriously as any couple I know. Throughout the many years I have known them, they have never wavered in their commitment to obey the command of Jesus to "make disciples who make disciples." When you read the stories he shares in *Living in the Overflow* and become privy to the passion of his heart, you will realize the blessings that accompany a sacrificial life and a generous heart.

Alton Garrison
Former Assistant General Superintendent
of the Assemblies of God

I met Mike Allard just after I became a Youth Pastor for Pastor J. Don George of Calvary Temple Church in Irving, Texas. I was a rookie and was invited to preach at the South Texas Youth Convention. I didn't know that one event would create a friend for a lifetime. Prior to coming to Cornerstone Church in Nashville I spent time in the evangelistic field and worked with Pastor Allard in both his role as Youth Pastor and then District Youth Director. I have traveled with Mike throughout the Southeastern parts of the United States, speaking in camps, churches and public schools as well as comprehensive travel throughout South Texas and internationally for missions work in Kenya. His passion for people is amazing and his capacity for creativity is abnormally large. Yet the greatest quality in Mike Allard is his ability to not quit in the hard times, to maintain a spirit of determination, faith and somehow to find humor that is unexpected and transformational in serious situations. His church is alive, his family is vibrant and I have never doubted that Mike is a friend that you could call at any time, under any circumstance and he would be there. This book I have no doubt is a faith builder, a hope giver and a book to bring healing to hurting hearts.

Maury Davis
President, Maury Davis Ministries

Pastor Mike Allard opens his heart and his own experience once again in the pages of this book. These are not just theological ideas or constructs, but real-life lessons gleaned from the pages of Scripture and his own walk with the Savior. If I had to choose one word to describe this man of God I would use the word "generous"! He preaches, teaches, leads and walks out of the principle that you can't outgive God. In the realm of world missions, Pastor Allard has made a deeply significant impact through the many missionaries the church supports monthly and through the Spirit-empowered and experienced teams they send out often to assist those same missionaries scattered around the globe. In just thinking about the FireBible ministry, Crossroads has helped to create and distribute more than 20 new language Bibles to leaders around the world, a huge investment on their part and one that is bringing dividends to the Body of Christ worldwide. Read and be inspired to go to another level of blessing and generosity in your own life.

Jeffrey W. Dove
Director,
Life Publishers International
The AG Bible Alliance (FireBible)

We have known Mike and Danielle Allard for 35 years. In that time I have watched their leadership abilities come alive with dignity and honesty above reproach. Their leadership as District Youth leaders for South Texas has not been matched. Mike is one of the premier speakers in mission events around the world. Danielle is Ms. Personality-Plus with people. She meets people of all nationalities with compassion and smiles that make her stand out as a woman of love and sweetness for all who meet her. Dee and I have had the honor to be close friends with the Allards and watch God use them in building one of America's great churches at Crossroads in Houston, Texas. Their love for the church as a whole is evident in the millions of dollars they have raised by their leadership at Crossroads. When you meet the Allards you will agree they are two of God's chosen.

Gary and Dee Sapp
Lead Pastors
Harvest Church
West Monroe, LA.

I have had the incredible joy of knowing Pastor Mike Allard for over 35 years, and from the first time we met years ago, it was obvious that this was a young man with a clear calling and a passion to make a difference in his life and ministry. I saw it in his heart and leadership as he was serving in New Mexico then as a youth pastor, and I've had the joy of watching his ministry continue to grow and develop over the years, always with a heart not only to serve well in his pastoral leadership, but to lead the people in his church to step into everything God desires. The contents of his new book, *"Living in the Overflow"* are no surprise to me! He has lived and taught these principles for years now, even as he was walking them out in his personal life and the mission of the church. And now, he is sharing them with us all as he calls us to live in God's plans for overflow. Thanks Mike for living this life and for inviting us all to join in on the journey. The adventures of overflow are our future and the fulfillment of God's desire for us all as we join in the cause of advancing the Kingdom!

Michael Dickenson
District Superintendent
New Mexico Assemblies of God

"Living in the Overflow" is more than a title of a book but a way of life for my friend in ministry, pastor and author Mike Allard. Mike's larger-than-life personality bubbles over from a heart after God and a love for people. His private altar through personal prayer and digging into the Word of God makes for a fruitful and exciting public life and ministry. Living life to the full, or as Jesus described "life more abundantly" is how Mike pursues his passion for Jesus. That passion is on full display in his love for his family, his church family and his enormous heart for global missions! We've laughed, cried, prayed and pursued God together and I can confidently say that you will not only enjoy the stories and lessons in the pages ahead of you but get ready to allow Jesus to overflow in you. God will do exceeding and abundantly above and beyond all that you ask and think. Prepare yourself to overflow!

Ron Heitman
Illinois District Assemblies of God
Assistant Superintendent,
Chicago Evangel Church, Lead Pastor

For 25 years we've gleaned from the overflow of Mike and Danielle's real-life stories of giving, going and generosity. The joy with which they follow Jesus and serve his church locally and globally is directly correlated to their giving. This book will not only make you laugh, but it will inspire and stretch you. Read with a readiness to respond to what the Spirit is prompting in you, knowing that God will never ask from you, what he will not give through you.

Rodney & Shannon Fouts
Senior Pastor
North Church
Oklahoma City

"My heart is overflowing
with a good theme;
I recite my composition
concerning the King;
My tongue *is* the pen
of a ready writer."
(Psalm 45:1 NKJV)

Danielle and I,
Partners in Life and Ministry for 40 years!

Opening Thoughts

What is your heart overflowing with? I have found my heart can overflow with a lot of things. It can overflow with laughter, weeping, joy, singing, mourning, hurt, anger, greed, love, jealousy and even pain. If we are not careful, good and bad can find a home in our hearts.

I have a friend whose name is Thomas. He has a laugh that can overtake a room. It would take some priming but once he gets to laughing, he overflows with such laughter that he almost passes out. Now that's a lot of laughter. Many have seen my son Michael David, when he gets tickled about a joke, sometime falls to the ground laughing. I've caught myself not really laughing at the joke but laughing with his laughter. It's contagious.

God has designed all of us like a vessel. To be full of something. The Psalmist in Psalm 45, says, "My heart is overflowing with a good theme; I'd like to tweak that with, "My heart is overflowing with a GOD theme." I want it to overflow with His themes.

What is Your Heart Overflowing With?

Psalm 45 is attributed to the sons of Korah. The same Korah who rebelled against Moses in the wilderness. You remember the story?

"Now it came to pass, as he finished speaking all these words, that the ground split apart under them, 32 and the earth opened its mouth and swallowed them up, with their households and all the men with Korah, with all *their* goods.

33 So they and all those with them went down alive into the pit; the earth closed over them, and they perished from among the assembly. 34 Then all Israel who *were* around them fled at their cry, for they said, "Lest the earth swallow us up *also!*" (Numbers 16:31-34 NKJV)

This scoundrel Korah is the great-great-grand father of the sons of Korah in the Psalms. You may have never put the two together. One is a very hostile, power-hungry man and the others are worshippers and writers of the Psalms. Can you imagine living down that legacy? Korah was such a vile person that the earth literally split open and swallowed him and all his rebels.

These were priests. The Kohathites were in charge of carrying the Ark of the Covenant. This family group of leaders was the upper end of the most honored priests. Numbers 4 says they were set apart for carrying holy things. How is it that such a holy group of men can find themselves so at odds with the man of God? Pride, arrogance, fear, hate, power, you name it... it could be any number of things that was driving Korah, and his rebellion.

Korah is like Adam. He was destroyed by his sin. However, we are called to carry the wonderful presence of the Lord. What a powerful responsibility for all of us as sons of Adam. This renewal comes through Christ. He is the second Adam. Because of His forgiveness and life, we have a second chance at fulfilling what God the Father wants us to do.

The beauty I found in this psalm is that the sons of Korah, at some point said, "We have to repent. We have a sacred duty. We can't let this same spirit of rebellion be in us. We must follow the Lord. We need the overflow of His presence in us, so we can minister, and carry the holy vessels." They could have had a hateful, nasty attitude of 'I'm going to get even,' but instead they write...

"My heart is overflowing with a good theme..."

For me, I have to join in that song and repeat it daily, Oh God, overflow in my life! Fill my emptiness. Let what comes out of me overflow from a heart of gratefulness and praise.

"My soul shall make its boast in the Lord; The humble shall hear *of it* and be glad. 3 Oh, magnify the Lord with me, and let us exalt His name together. 4 I sought the Lord, and He heard me, and delivered me from all my fears." (Psalm 34:2-4 NKJV)

I've said it, over and over...

Real MINISTRY comes out of the OVERFLOW!

Let the theme of my life overflow with your presence. Let it fill every part of my day. Every conversation, every thought, and every place I go, let it be that I overflow with you Lord!

My desire is as you read *"Living in the Overflow" you will not think in terms* of what am I receiving or will receive but what can I give? What can I give to make Christ more real? What is overflowing in me that can overflow to someone else?

Ezekiel 47:9 NKJV
*"And it shall be that every living thing that moves,
wherever the rivers go, will live."*

The waterfall at Ein Gedi, Israel

Chapter 1

Living in the Overflow!

The Best OVERFLOW Comes from the Lord!

"My heart is overflowing with a good theme; I recite my composition concerning the King; My tongue *is* the pen of a ready writer." (Psalm 45:1 NKJV)

O ur greatest ministry begins where the darkest need exists. Overflow reaches where human effort stops. It pours out of a heart full of God's love. We release the aroma of worship as we live in His overflow of love. We must allow it to spill over from the ordinary to become the extraordinary!

Psalm 45 declares my heart is OVERFLOWING with a good theme. A good theme sounds amazing! A God theme sounds even better! It sounds inspiring. Many people have never found that moment. That place where God touches your heart and it overflows with His theme.

What is the theme of your life?
If your life were a movie what would it be about?
Would it be a comedy or a tragedy?
Would the theme be about you giving or taking?
Would it be about what you earned and became or what you gave and sacrificed?
What is your theme?

If my life could be a stream of helping and inspiring others I would say that was a God theme! God's themes are the best themes! God has a theme for all of us. I like to call it purpose. In a hundred years what would I find if I googled your name?

What would be the top five words that would be associated with your name for someone to find you? What five words would you choose? Just five words to find you and I need to know what would those words be? You might say, "that's hard." It's probably not but whatever overflows in my life will forever be associated with my name.

So, I want to live my life with purpose. I want to live my life on purpose. With a GREAT cause at the center of my life.

What would the accumulation of your life be if it were made into one sentence? Not a paragraph but a sentence.

Jim Elliot was an evangelical Christian who was one of five missionaries killed while participating in Operation Auca, an attempt to evangelize the Huaorani people of Ecuador. He was martyred on January 8, 1956.

Because Jim Elliot was consumed with the Great Commission

he overflowed with Christ's love to reach an unreached people group.

In Jim's diary entry dated October 28, 1949, Jim wrote this sentence. *"He is no fool who gives what he cannot keep to gain that which he cannot lose."* That's a life theme. A picture of a person sold out for Christ.

Not many people write out their life theme in advance of living it. They will normally live through something and then the theme seems to come forth. When I first started writing this book I was consumed with the thought of the overflow and really hadn't given much thought of a life theme. My life theme has become Never Give Up! At the darkest time of my life I truly wanted to quit. I wanted to give up *BUT GOD WOULD NOT LET ME!*

So, I live now to encourage others. I'm not always good at it. Perhaps I'm an encourager in training.

A great way to know your life's theme is to ask yourself, "What does my life overflow with?" Some people have lived a powerful life theme.

Here are a few "note-able" life themes:

Martin Luther King Jr. - "I have a dream!"
Patrick Henry - "Give me liberty or give me death!"
The Apostle Paul - "To live is Christ to die is gain."
The Apostle Peter - "Thou art the Christ the son of the living God"
Joshua - "As for me and my house we will serve the Lord"
Mother Teresa - "Your true character is most accurately measured by how you treat those who can do nothing for you."

So, What's Your Life's Theme?

I'll give you a clue. You've already been writing it. It's what you do every day. It's what you live for and where you go and how you spend your money. It's the value you put in what you do. It's what you would probably die for.

For many of us, we've become so accustomed to asking our assistant Siri or googling a few words to find out the information we're looking for. Usually it takes four or five key words and you can find a person, place or thing really fast. I began thinking if my life were just five words what would those words be? Pastor, friend, missions, father, husband, hunter, artist, writer, crossroads, generous, etc. Sorry - that's ten.

What would be your five?

Could those five words become the soul of a sentence that would be reflective of who you are? This is the theme of your life. Your life has a theme. What does it overflow with? If you were to ask someone who is close to you what would be their five words to describe you? What would they say? The answer might surprise you.

Here is a great daily theme for living life. I would even describe it as a life scripture. A way to live and let one's life overflow with blessing.

Called to Bless and Be a Blessing

"[8] Finally, all *of you be* of one mind, having compassion for one another; love as brothers, *be* tenderhearted, *be* courteous; [9] not returning evil for evil or reviling for reviling, but on the contrary blessing, knowing that you were called to this, that you may inherit a blessing. [10] For "He who would love life and see good days, let him refrain his tongue from evil, and his lips from speaking deceit. [11] Let him turn away from evil and do good; Let him seek peace and pursue it. [12] For the eyes of the Lord *are* on the righteous, And His ears *are open* to their prayers; But the face of the Lord *is* against those who do evil." (1 Peter 3:8-12 NKJV)

Andrew

There's a young man in our church. His name is Andrew. Andrew is one of the sweetest young men you could ever meet. He and his brother Brandon were born twins at 26 weeks. Andrew weighed 2 pounds, 10 ounces and was 14 inches long at birth. When he was about a month old he contracted spinal meningitis while still in the NICU. The meningitis scarred the part of his brain that reabsorbs cerebrospinal fluid (CSF). His brain thought it wasn't producing enough because none was being reabsorbed. (It's a recycling process.) His brain started producing more CSF. He developed hydrocephalus, a build up of fluid in the cavities deep within the brain. The additional fluid started squeezing his brain. He started having seizures. They did emergency surgery to put in an Omaha reservoir. It allowed them to pull out excess CSF without going into his ventricles. He came home when he was six months old. His parents had to take him to the hospital twice a week to have fluid removed. He's had a total of eleven brain surgeries and currently has two ventro-peritoneal shunts in place. They automatically drain the CSF to his abdomen.

To read that you think what a terrible, hopeless situation. But God is a God of love and answers prayer. Andrew was very young when he, Brandon, his Dad and Mom Jonathan and Laura, and his two sisters Christian and Delaney started attending Crossroads. He and Brandon were around seven.

He's now twenty-five. For all the years I've known this family, they have declared over Andrew and Brandon healing, life and the power of Christ. Unfortunately, Brandon passed away a few years back due to complications with his breathing device. But Andrew has steadily gotten better and better. The doctors said Andrew would never walk or talk. He should have lived his life in a vegetative state, but God touched him. He is a walking, talking miracle, and sometimes that miracle talks too much (haha). He truly is a miracle! Today, he quotes Scripture more than most faithful church members. Yet Andrew cannot read. He is always at the church. He constantly listens to

Scripture and preaching. In fact, Andrew tells me quite often, "Pastor, if you need some good preaching, I've got some I'm listening to. It might help you!" Andrew is the only person who can get away with that, if you know what I mean. He had terrible seizures for the first ten years of his life. He rarely has even a mild seizure now. They said he would need frequent surgeries as he grew to replace the shunt. He hasn't had another surgery since he was very young.

During my early morning prayer times at the church, Andrew and his parents will come quite frequently, and he will usually sit just a couple chairs from where I sit and on the same row and pray. While the prayer music is playing Andrew will pray. He also likes to sing (off key), There have been days while he is praying I find myself listening to what Andrew is praying. He prays with such sincerity and power. He really loves the Lord with all of his heart. One morning I heard him say, "Bless the Lord of <u>ALL</u> my soul!" Let that sink in. Wow! That's pretty good I thought to myself. <u>Bless the Lord of **ALL** my soul</u>. Not holding anything back. You've got ALL of me, God! That's Andrew, completely and entirely.

You see, Andrew has a theme to his life. He loves the Lord. He loves everything about the Lord. His love for the Lord is a love that his parents have cultivated. They didn't take a bad doctor's report as the final diagnosis. That would have been easy. They have believed for his complete healing and all of his cognitive abilities to be fully functional. They have loved and have instilled a **GOD THEME** in Andrew.

Don't get me wrong Andrew is by no means perfect. Many times, Andrew will "amen" me at the wrong time. Sometimes he will answer rhetorical questions during the middle of a sermon, OUT LOUD! One day I asked, trying to get some point across to the crowd about excitement and using the Houston Astros as an example, I said, *"Why do we go see the Astros play?"* (meaning the excitement of the game). But before I knew it, Andrew answered, (in his best Forrest Gump-like voice he replied), <u>"To watch them lose!"</u> Of course, that drew a big laugh from the audience. He loves it when he makes everyone laugh. I had to tell him that day, *"Look Andrew, I work alone!"*

The wonderful thing about Andrew is he's getting better and better. He is no longer functioning on a child's level. He sees and understands. His parents were told he would never be able to remember things. But he quotes Scripture completely from memory.

One day I asked Andrew, "How did you get so smart?" His reply: "GOD TAUGHT ME!"

Andrew now works helping his Dad in his IT business. He helps doing little things. He is primarily his Dad's chief encourager. He rides along in the truck. He gives a little advice here and there and carries things and helps pull wire and makes funny wisecracks. But, every day he and his Dad have a declaration that they say together.

"I'm quick, bright, sharp, very good-looking and a major blessing to all those around me."

Andrew is a beautiful picture of a GOD-THEMED life living in the overflow. He's awesome. I get to be his friend. He loves to have fun. He laughs about a lot of stuff. But his life overflows with pure love for the Lord and others. If only we all could be more like Andrew!

"Death and life are in the power of the tongue, and those who love it will eat its fruits." (Proverbs 18:21 ESV)

If you ever come to Crossroads, you'll get to meet Andrew, because Andrew works as one of our greeters. He's pretty amazing! He's got a big beard and smiles a lot.

He's definitely living in the overflow, and WE LOVE HIM!

Spillways

Thinking of overflow makes me think of a spillway. I've driven over many concrete spillways in my truck. They are designed in such a way as to allow water to gradually make its way over.

As I thought about this I thought about how we have spillways in our lives. Positive spillways of love, joy, praise, gratitude, and negative spillways of anger, hate, vice, lust, fear, greed etc. When the spillway of love is overflowing then hugs, kisses, and kindness flow. When the spillway of hatred has reached its limit, it might overflow with cursing and a slap.

The first question is, what are you filling up with? You can give yourself a test. Ask yourself, "What's been spilling out of me?" What are others experiencing from me? What would my spouse say?

How about your kids? What, would their answer be? Perhaps a friend could tell you. I believe it's whatever you have been filling up on. Love, joy, peace, longsuffering, kindness, goodness, faithfulness, gentleness and self-control overflow from a heart full of the Holy Spirit. Maybe you've been filling up on Netflix or Hulu or social media like FaceBook. That's what will pour out of you. Whatever you've been putting in.

Water and More Water

If you live on the Texas coast for any length of time, at some point you will experience a tropical storm or a hurricane. In

2017 we had a once-in-a-generation storm named Hurricane Harvey. He was relentless. The rain totals from this storm were in a class all their own. Harvey unloaded over 50 inches of rain on Houston, the greatest amount ever recorded in the lower 48 states from a single storm.

The average rainfall in Houston per year is 49.76 inches. So imagine, in just a few days Houston was overflowing with a year's worth of rain. 1961 was the last time a Category 4 hurricane (Carla) had hit the central coast of Texas. Every bayou, river, creek and canal overflowed with unbelievable amounts of water. Areas that had never flooded were overcome with the deluge of unwanted water. Many neighborhoods had to evacuate. People in rafts and boats were seen carrying what little they could to get to dry ground. Many lost everything. As of 2020, some are still trying to get life back to normal.

Families evacuated flooded neighborhoods near our church during Hurricane Harvey.

"You Won't Believe This…"

As the flooding of Hurricane Harvey was happening a friend of mine who works at the Coastal Water Authority asked me if I wanted to come and see the flow of water over the spillway. It was definitely a strange request but it sounded interesting. He said, "You won't believe this, it's huge. I've worked here for over thirty years and I've never seen it like this."

So, here I am surrounded by a flood and my buddy wants me to come look at more water. To give you an idea of the flooding in downtown Houston bayous during Harvey, the following pictures were shared on social media. It's the dramatic difference of two days of severe flooding and what can happen when 50 inches of rain descend upon a major metropolitan area. Our bayous could not contain the massive amounts of water.

A Category 4 hurricane, Harvey was the first major hurricane in 56 years to hit the Texas central coast.
Not since Hurricane Carla in 1961 had the region received a direct hit from a Category 4 storm.

Because we were flooded in, our son Joshua had to come and get us with his boat. It was truly surreal moment as we were picked up at the front door of our home. We were amazed at the level of the flooding. Even though we were spared the flood waters in our home we saw many homes on the way out that were sadly not spared.

When we arrived at the Lake Houston spillway we could hear it before we saw it. The flood waters were ten feet above the spillway. The sight was absolutely amazing. Millions of gallons of water were rushing over the edge and crashing below. The sound was deafening. It was overflowing unlike anything I had ever seen in my lifetime. Powerful! Amazing! Breathtaking! Overwhelming!

Spillways of the Holy Spirit

What if we had an OVERFLOW of God's precious Holy Spirit in our lives like that? Pouring over the spillway of our hearts. Unable to keep it in. Just pouring out to everyone we meet. A joy that is full and powerful. What if His presence was so genuine and fresh that everyone we met would feel that same refreshing power? His presence brings life to all who come in contact with it. All the hurting would feel refreshed!

Spillways of Trouble

When Tropical Storm Allison hit in 2001, it arrived the very first week I became pastor at Crossroads Fellowship. Allison dumped over 40 inches of water on Houston in a very short amount of time. Thousands became homeless after the storm flooded over 70,000 houses and destroyed 2,744 homes. The horrific event was one of the most devastating water deluges in recorded American history. This five-hundred-year flood destroyed thirty-five homes in our church family. With a church of a few hundred people and each family having an average of three people that meant that a huge percentage of our church family was hurting and devastated.

Spillways of Ministry

It was a mess. Everything was a mess! Overflowing in water and gunk! A lot of nasty-smelly gunk! On top of that I had started a forty-day fast on the first day I started pastoring. I told the Lord, "I'm giving you these first forty days. I'm setting my heart on you!"

Then this disaster struck. What? Why? Hey God, I'm trying to be spiritual and fast! You can stop the rain!

A few weeks after this storm hit, a good friend of mine, Dr. Paul Ai, called me and asked how was I doing? I told him, "Terrible, I'm in the aftermath of this flood. I am so busy and exhausted." He told me that within his Asian culture rain is a sign of blessing. "With that much rain God must be getting ready to bless you in a big way," he said. At the time I didn't think like that, but I do like the way he framed that for me. *"God must be getting ready to bless you in a big way."* Little did I realize, at the time, how much of a blessing that flood was. It was such a blessing that I was able to be in thirty-five homes immediately helping thirty-five families.

The Blessing of a Crisis

It was horrible and yet a wonderful blessing. We got to reach many hurting people. They were devastated and we became an instrument in God's hand. We were able to bring needed relief. It was wonderful. In God's plan for me, it created an opportunity for me to be with all the busted and broken families. God didn't cause the crisis, but God used the crisis to make ministry happen. When the enemy tears and rips people apart it's an open door for someone to walk in with God's love and bring healing. It was like what Joseph told his brothers in

Genesis 50:20a "But as for you, you meant evil against me; <u>but God meant it for good</u>." God turned it around for good! God used the crisis to pull our church together to reach out and minister. That kind of overflow wasn't what we were looking for but there was an overflow of ministry that was given. It was a different kind of unexpected living in the overflow.

Love Others

The Wednesday night before Allison hit was June 5, 2001. That night I preached out of the book of Isaiah... *"Is* this not the fast that I have chosen: To loose the bonds of wickedness, To undo the heavy burdens, To let the oppressed go free, And that you break every yoke? [7] *Is it* not to share your bread with the hungry, And that you bring to your house the poor who are cast out; When you see the naked, that you cover him, And not hide yourself from your own flesh? [8] Then your light shall break forth like the morning, Your healing shall spring forth speedily, And your righteousness shall go before you; The glory of the Lord shall be your rear guard. [9] Then you shall call, and the Lord will answer; You shall cry, and He will say, 'Here I *am...*'" (Isaiah 58:6-9 NKJV)

In that sermon I remember saying, "One day, Convoy of Hope will be in our parking lot ministering to our community." Little did I know, the next week Convoy of Hope would be there, in our parking lot, with tractor trailers full of supplies, and the Coast Guard would be dropping people into our parking lot, and our gymnasium would become a homeless shelter. It was amazing! It was Isaiah 58 fulfilled right before our eyes.

What Happened?

That overflow of disaster turned into an overflow of ministry to our community.

Our gymnasium became a shelter for the homeless.
300 people from our community moved in. That meant our church really more than doubled overnight.
We grew closer as a church.
We needed each other.
We fed the hungry.
We clothed the naked.
We distributed cleaning supplies to hurting people.
We helped families dig out of the mess.
We rebuilt homes.
We gave.
We cooked meals.
We prayed.
We reported the stories of survival.
We shared pictures and felt overwhelmed at times.
We eventually laughed and sang.
We celebrated the victories and cried over the losses.
And the list goes on and on!
Sometimes the greatest moment is the crisis, when the opportunity to be a blessing is right in front of you. None of us want to experience a disaster but bad things do happen.

In that moment, we pulled together. We lifted each other. We carried each other's burdens. So, whether it's happening to you or someone else it can be a great opportunity to let His love flow through you.

How Do You Handle Blessings?

I can't think of anyone not wanting to live a great life! It's true. When others see how you live life in the hard times, it causes them to want to serve Christ also. However, not only is it how you live in the bad times others need to see. <u>It's how you live in the good times</u>. When you've got plenty. When you seemingly don't need God. When the money is knee deep and your job is great. How do you live then? Do you serve faithfully? Do you pray fervently? Do you give generously? Do you love everyone the same? Have you become a snob? Do you act like the world owes you MORE? But living in the overflow is not about having more finances. More finances is a result of obedience to God's covenant of tithes and generosity.

Enjoy the Journey

Too many times we are waiting, wanting and wishing some day in the future to get here. We miss what God is trying to do now. He wants His amazing love to flow through us. We end up missing the journey. The Swahili word for journey is "safari." I've been on several African picture safaris. You travel in these open vehicles and you take pictures of the animals. You want to remember all the things you see. The lion cubs, the zebras, wildebeests, elephants, hippos, and rhinos. It's wonderful. You and I are on a great safari called life. Enjoy your safari. Take a deep breath. That is God's breath that flows through your body. It started when God first breathed life into Adam and Eve, and they became living souls, and it continues today, with you and me. Living life in the overflow is stopping and seeing life. Enjoying the moments. Look at the sights and the colors each day has to offer. We're not promised tomorrow and so today is it. Don't blow it. The next twenty-four hours is a wonderful gift. If that was all you had what would you do with it? How will you make it count?

"So, teach *us* to number our days, that we may gain a heart of wisdom." (Psalm 90:12 NKJV)

The overflow is where we should parent from. It's being a better spouse and serving with all your heart, in the church and at your job. It's being generous with your life. It's time to face the hard truth and deal with it. Get victory over the petty things that are driving you crazy and LIVE!

The overflow starts at the beginning of every day. It's getting up and thanking the Lord. For me, it's the recognition that I have breath and I can walk and there is a beautiful family that loves me and why shouldn't I try harder to be better? It's counting the small things as favor and God's goodness. It's that first hour in the presence of the Lord. It's the overflowing in the Spirit and allowing that same Holy Spirit to speak through me to a lonely, broken world.

It's looking for a better path. It's bringing the oasis to someone who needs a drink. Maybe it's in the smile and laughter of a child, or perhaps it's watching someone grab hold of a great truth. It's celebrating a new believer's FREEDOM in Christ. I believe through the reading of this book you will discover the joy of Living in the OVERFLOW! And I pray when you do that, you will share it with someone else.

Enjoy Your Life's Safari
Nellie and I in Africa

Study Guide Chapter 1

Living in the Overflow
The Best OVERFLOW Comes from the Lord!

"My heart is overflowing with <u>a good theme</u>; I recite my composition concerning the King; My tongue is the pen of a ready writer."   (Psalm 45:1 NKJV)

Our greatest ministry begins where the darkest need exists. Overflow reaches where human effort stops. It pours out of a heart full of God's love. We release the aroma of worship as we live in His overflow of love. We must allow it to spill over from the ordinary to become the extraordinary!

What is the theme of your life?
e.g., kids, work, marriage, hobby, ministry, other, etc.

_____

_____

_____

_____

_____

_____

_____

What are your five words?
1._____
2._____
3._____
4._____
5._____

What is a spillway in your life?
A spillway is something you give freely to.

_____

_____

_____

How do you tend to handle crisis? (you can check more than one)
Complain _____ Rejoice_____ Fear_____ Opportunity_____
Pray_____ Encourage_____Withdraw_____ Give_____
Blame_____ Overreact_____ Fight_____Help_____Cry_____

Describe a crisis that God turned into good?
e.g., flat tire, a bill paid, wreck, fire, sickness, storm, etc.

_____

_____

_____

_____

_____

_____

Romans 8:28 MEV
"We know that all things work together for good to those who love God, to those who are called according to His purpose."

Exodus 50:20 MEV
"But as for you, you intended to harm me, but God intended it for good, in order to bring it about as it is this day, to save many lives."

What are some great pictures in your life's safari?

_____

_____

_____
_____

Psalm 90:12 NKJV
"So, teach us to number our days, that we may gain a heart of wisdom."

Jeremiah 29:11 MEV
"For I know the plans that I have for you, says the Lord, plans for peace and not for evil, to give you a future and a hope."

If you could change anything in the future what would it be? What will you do differently?

_____
_____
_____
_____
_____

Psalm 37:23 NKJV
"The steps of a good man are ordered by the Lord, And He delights in his way."

Psalm 119:2 MEV
"Blessed are those who keep His testimonies, and who seek
Him with all their heart."

I took this picture at the Wailing Wall in Jerusalem.

Jeremiah 1:4-5 NKJV

"Then the word of the Lord came to me, saying: 'Before I formed you in the womb I knew you; Before you were born I sanctified you; I ordained you a prophet to the nations.'"

My son Joshua leading worship in Vietnam.

Chapter 2

Just Enough or More Than Enough?

"Full of Nothing!"

"Be anxious for nothing, but in everything by prayer and supplication, with thanksgiving, let your requests be made known to God;" (Philippians 4:6 NKJV)

Have you ever had just enough money to buy something? Perhaps you dropped into a convenience store to buy a coke and discovered you were short a nickel or a penny? Thankfully they have that little extra change dish. Some kind person left you a coin or two to help you out.

As a kid I grew up in a world of NOT ENOUGH! It seemed we lived on less-than-enough or barely enough. Many people today live from paycheck to paycheck. They wish for JUST ENOUGH to make it.

I remember, after Daddy left, Momma became the main breadwinner. She didn't make a lot of money. She worked as a bookkeeper, and most of the time she earned just enough. Sometimes it was not enough. I remember her sharing one time, years later, that it was around $350 a month she made and the mortgage was about half of that. How did she make it? She never complained, but she did tell us on many occasions, "It's tight, boys." That was the early 1970s.

The NOT ENOUGH we lived in was real. She would say, "I've got $10 between now and next payday." Those were days you bought school clothes once a year and they had to last. By the time May rolled around my toes were poking through my Chuck Taylors. I was fortunate to have one pair of "church shoes" and one pair of tennis shoes. Sometimes, I didn't have church shoes. Mom would buy me a few pair of jeans at the beginning of the school year. She'd get the kind with double knees. "Those were the best." That's what she said – toughskins, sold by Sears. Holes in your pants were not in style then. But occasionally I'd bust through even the toughskins. I guess they weren't so tough.

We didn't have central air in our home. That would be much later in life. I only remember Momma buying a few window units, when I was around seventeen. Some summers it seemed to stay over 100 degrees outside and it wasn't much cooler inside. You would melt in your socks, if you wore them... a lot of days, we just went barefoot. Those blazing hot summers, in Wichita Falls, we would open windows and use an old swamp cooler, and a couple of box fans, to try and get some relief. It wasn't enough to really keep you cool or keep you from feeling like you would die. It just moved the warm air around.

We prayed for rain! We needed an overflow from heaven to come and cool things off. One time, it rained and there was so much dirt in the air that it came down in mud balls. We needed rain but not mud rain! Haha!

Al, Bubba, and Mark were my childhood buddies and we would go to the Wichita River and swim. There was an old abandoned oil derrick down by the river and we would swing from a rope and enjoy its cool, refreshing waters. It was amazing! As a kid you could forget about the heat and all that. Sweat and stink was just how you lived. Most days we would have a row of dirt beads around our necks. We'd mow some lawns and earn a dollar or two. Every once in a while, we'd walk a couple of miles to the Sand's Motel on Seymour Highway and pay a buck to swim in a real swimming pool. You could stay all day. That was living!

In some ways, those were really great days. You didn't have to have a lot of stuff to enjoy life… but we made the most of what we had. We weren't the poorest family but we were near the bottom. We could definitely see where "the poor people lived."

Rejoice!

Momma later said, "We could have qualified for government money." But we didn't know about stuff like that. We just lived through it and we survived. Momma prayed, blessings came, and it seemed like as though we had a good-enough life. She was awesome! I wished I had known how special those days were. I would have told Mom I loved her a whole bunch more.

I remember her singing in the car. That old '64 Impala was a great ride. She was always singing when she took me to church or other places. She overflowed with praise to the Lord. In the midst of trouble and heartache! She would rejoice in the Lord. It reminds me of Paul's words to the Philippians…

"Rejoice in the Lord always. Again, I will say, rejoice! [5] Let your gentleness be known to all men. The Lord *is* at hand. [6] Be anxious for nothing, but in everything by prayer and supplication, with thanksgiving, let your requests be made known to God; [7] and the peace of God, which surpasses all understanding, will guard your hearts and minds through Christ Jesus." (Philippians 4:4-7 NKJV)

She rejoiced when she didn't seem to have anything to rejoice about. Rejoicing in the Lord is being joyful in Him, even when you don't have anything to be happy about. When it was tough. When it was hard. When things weren't going her way, I'd watch her still have a song. Don't get me wrong; I saw her down many times, but she would ultimately let the joy of the Lord fill her heart.

Live in the Overflow

She lived in the overflow. She was a great example in the land of not enough. Even though we didn't have material things, we had the Lord. We had family. We had the promises of God. And the Lord was our help!

"The name of the Lord *is* a strong tower; The righteous run to it and are safe." (Proverbs 18:10 NKJV)

It's sad to see how some people live. I'm not talking about the poor. It's heartbreaking to see people live in physical poverty. But I'm speaking of those who live in the poverty of the soul. They have plenty of stuff to fill their day, yet they are living on empty. The abundance of gadgets and devices never represses their hunger. They are always buying and never full. The emptiness is killing them. They've tried everything.

If You Knew...

In John, 4, we find the perfect picture of thirst and the need for His overflow. We don't know all the details, but we understand Jesus has stopped at Jacob's well in Sychar. He has sent his disciples to find provisions. It's in the middle of a very hot day. And there He meets a woman. He's thirsty and asks her for a drink of water. It seemed strange to her that He would even talk to her. She's been asked by a lot of men for things. But this is a simple drink of water. It is to quench the thirst of the Savior. Perhaps she thinks He is like all the other men. Out for their needs only - forget her and her desperation. Who cares what she needs? The Savior doesn't miss a wonderful opportunity to help a thirsty soul. "If you knew who it was that's asking of you a drink you would ask of Me and I would give you the water of life freely." (John 4:10) She's puzzled. Why do you speak to me? I'm a Samaritan and you are a Jew. How can you draw water? You don't have anything to draw with. You say we should worship there, and we say here. Isn't that like human nature? We have the greatest answer to life right in front of us and we question the gift of God's amazing love. We even question the motive of God's love.

Jesus Lived in the Overflow

Jesus spoke to her and told her to go get her husband. He already knew that she'd had five husbands and the guy she was shacking up with wasn't her husband. Her life was filled with emptiness. It was written all over her face. Her life represented a person who had tried everything, every kind of relationship. She's now coming to draw water at the hottest part of the day. Was it because she was scorned for her lifestyle? Was it because she had slept late, because of her late-night activities or because the Holy Spirit had set her up, to have this wonderful encounter in the middle of the day with Jesus? I like to think it might have been all three. Wow! Here Christ stops and sits and talks with this 100% unworthy sinner. She is lost! She is to the core not religious and right with God. She's not even a Jew. She's a so-called "half-breed." She's lacking all the credentials for this meeting. She's made no appointment. Only that they casually meet at this well. A place of refreshing. That's where you can find Him today. At the well of refreshing.

Wanting to refresh and replenish the thirsty. Yet what He gives will satisfy forever. We've had so many chance meetings with the thirsty of this world. How many times have we avoided conversations? How many times have we missed the moment Christ gave His life for? Freely we have received but do we freely give?

Even in His tiredness and resting He found opportunity to give of Himself. He saw her need. Someone's need brought life to Him. He saw her thirst. He recognized her need. Not as an intrusion on His day but as a God moment to minister to the hurting. He was living in the overflow!

What If?

What if we lived in the overflow? What if we lived like that? What if we recognized situations and circumstances as opportunities, not as problems or diversions from our precious plans and set schedules. What if we allowed the Holy Spirit to put some things on our schedule so the overflow of His presence can meet someone else's need? What if we could just stop and see the thirsty and hungry needing a word of encouragement? What if we responded by joyfully providing a little ministry in the heat of the day.

Full of Nothing

Unfortunately, many pastors and Christians minister out of the just enough. They are overloaded and overwhelmed with too much. They are burned out and have nothing to give. No need to dig anymore for a sermon. So they take advantage of sermon services who will gladly write a sermon for a monthly fee. *They are full of nothing.* Exhaustion is in the bottom of their life. They haven't felt a fresh infusion of God's overflow in a long time. In fact, they are parched and dry. Oh

Father, fill the hungry! Fill the men and women of God who carry so much! To many times we lean on the next cool idea and not the flow of His presence. God give us more of you! Let us not avoid and be distracted by a full schedule, not to stop and give our time and love to the most unworthy. To the person who has so little to offer. May your love overflow from us to them. Help us!

How can we give to the world of "Not Enough" when we have barely enough? If the leader doesn't have enough, how will the church?

Just Enough

So many people live in that land of spiritual just enough. They have just enough of Jesus to feel okay, most of the time. They have just enough of Jesus to keep the preacher away. It might appear they have a real relationship with the Lord, but they have never experienced the overflow of HIS AMAZING LOVE! They pray just enough to say they've prayed. Just enough attendance to church. Just enough religion to inoculate them from the real Jesus.

The church is the Bride of Christ. What groom is hoping for a bride that has just enough love that she won't leave him? That she won't wink at secret lover, when he's not watching. Christ wants a genuine relationship with all who will accept Him as Savior. Paul tells the Ephesian believers "that Christ may dwell in your hearts through faith; that you, being rooted and grounded in love, [18] may be able to comprehend with all the saints what *is* the width and length and depth and height— [19] to know the love of Christ which passes knowledge; that you may be filled with all the fullness of God." (Ephesians 3:17-19 NKJV)

That's understanding the life of the overflow. When you've walked the width and length and depth and climbed the height of His love. When you realize you can't even begin to understand how great it is. That's being filled with the fullness of God - living in the overflow. When you've received so much you have to give it away to someone else, so they can carry on and love as you are loved. When you realize it'll take a thousand lifetimes to even begin to try to and repay the great gift of His amazing grace. But there's no way to even start to repay what He has done for us! So, give it away to everyone you meet. Remember, it was Christ who walked that love out with you. He didn't give up on you. He was a patient shepherd. He sent a bunch of people your way and now you are one He sends to someone who needs to receive. Let it overflow through you.

Give it Away

Many have never heard of His saving love. They live in the world of not enough. Not enough love, not enough peace, not enough rest, not enough joy, not enough care or happiness. They live in the darkest places. The places where the light of God's love has never been received. We've been given a Great Commission to take that love there. Let it overflow from your heart to those in need. Give it away! Give all of it away! Let your life become a channel of His love! Strip away the ropes of care and worry. Let His perfect love steady you. Listen to Him, listen to His direction. Give!

Give the overflow free flow through your life.

More Than Enough

"Freely you have received, freely give." (Matthew 10:8 NKJV)

What keeps us from giving? What dams up our heart to share? What hinders a loving overflow of God's love? Is it our pride? Is it greed? Perhaps a selfish heart? Over my years on this Earth I've come to understand a law about giving in the overflow. This is that law: *When you feel the tug to give, then give! Give it then and give it gladly!*

Kaijado

I stood there in the bright Kenyan sunlight.
"How much would it cost to give this village free water for life?"

We were standing in the Kenyan village of Kaijado. I asked the question when I addressed the pastor of the Kenyan Assembly of God Church, Joshua Kotoke. I had noticed people standing in line to buy water at the church well. There were mothers, fathers, and children of every age and size standing and holding a variety of containers waiting to be filled. To me it seemed strange to see people waiting for water and needing to pay for it, especially at a village church.

I grew up drinking from a water hose. Playing ball with my buddiess and running in the house putting my mouth on the faucet because I was so thirsty I couldn't grab a glass first. I'm old enough to remember the first time I saw water for sale in a bottle. I thought how strange this is! No one will ever buy water. Water is free! Yet, in 2017 391 billion liters of water were sold in the world.[1] To me, water is a basic need that everyone should have met. At my home water flows freely. Sure, there's a price in a bill that comes once a month. The cost is minimal. But here in the African slum of Kaijado, it is costly. It may seem like a few shillings but to the poor there is a genuine cost. We live in a land of MORE THAN ENOUGH! How can we hold back from the world of NOT ENOUGH?

An Oasis in the Desert

The church in Kaijado is an oasis of sorts in a desert of small shanty houses and dung huts. We've been going there since 2014. We go to the village to minister to the hurting. Many of our Crossroads members sponsor children through One Child Matters. It has become an annual trip to the country to see them and bring encouragement.

"Pure and undefiled religion before God and the Father is this: to visit orphans and widows in their trouble, *and* to keep oneself unspotted from the world. (James 1:27 NKJV)

---

1. https://www.statista.com/statistics/387255/global-bottled-water-consumption/

I watched in the warm sun as they shuffled to the spigot at the little tin-roof-enclosed well. The water tower, not more than thirty feet high and holding a few thousand gallons of water, was systematically released as each vessel would be placed under the spout. An attendant opened the valve, releasing the precious, cool, refreshing water. Then the person would pay and carry their filled vessel home. Children struggled under the weight of their families, needed refreshment, an essential for life. It was a slow process but what a picture of thirst and it being quenched.

I called the people standing in line there to come near. There were probably twenty to thirty waiting with their containers. Some of them had old plastic oil bottles, anti-freeze jugs, gas cans and grease containers, I even saw one holding a battery acid jug (I hope it was washed out first). All were waiting for their containers to be filled to the brim to take home. All desired refreshing water for their families.

"Listen, everyone..."

I called to them to attention. I announced that I had spoken to the pastor of the church and as I spoke, I felt a breaking in my voice. It was the emotion of the moment. I went on to say,

"We agreed that our church would pay the price each month from now on for them to have FREE WATER FOR LIFE!" No one will ever have to pay for water, ever again, at this well.

There was a pause at first, then there was a startled look by the listeners. The interpreter spoke the words clearly now. A lady gave out a loud tongue-wiggling whoop and then the crowd began to clap and applaud. It was a wonderful moment. For our church it represented a $500-a-month commitment. It was small in comparison, in cost to us, but it was great in value to the thirsty of Kaijado. It was a game-changer for the village.

See the Need

Living in the overflow is looking for the simple, everyday thing you can do to make a difference. It may seem like a simple thing to you but for someone else, it may change their life forever. Your overflow of love might be what somebody needs just to make it. Ask the Lord to lead you and to make you sensitive to the little things people say. It might change them, and it will definitely change you.

Give!

Each jug of water represented a few shillings to the church, but it helped the church with their budget. To me as I stood there, it was the Holy Spirit speaking that overflowed in my heart. Give! How many times have I felt His tug at my heart?

Over the years I've learned that need is one of the greatest gifts He gives me every day. The need of someone else is His way of reminding me I am blessed, and that I am called to be a blessing.

Think about this. If you have $10 in your pocket, you have more money than 80% of the world's population. That means you have more wealth than six billion people in the world. Wow! You are pretty rich!

Most of the world exists in poverty and struggles from day to day. They live from hand to mouth on whatever they can find. They scratch out barely enough to make ends meet. They might have one meal a day. We will have at least three meals most days, and those will most likely be large portions. Living in the land of More would be their grandest dream. They would be happy with just enough, but more would be impossible.

You may be a single parent with two kids. You probably have a whole list of bills to pay: rent; doctors; school; groceries; repairs; clothes; car payment and there's nothing extra you can afford. You can live in the overflow also. My mom was joyful in the midst of poverty. She was like the widow with two mites. What she had was all she had, and she was always willing to share what she had.

Many times, we had aunts, cousins and others come and stay at our home. Eat at our table and enjoy what we had, and we didn't really have it to spare. When I was just a boy, God used Momma to demonstrate the overflow and the joy of giving.

"For everyone to whom much is given, from him much will be required; and to whom much has been committed, of him they will ask the more." (Luke 12:48b NKJV)

Several years ago, a single mom came to our church. She was living in extreme poverty. Her two boys were all she had after a tragic divorce due to her former husband's drug addiction. We loved on them and received them gladly into our fellowship. Her name is Catherine Garcia, and we call her

"Cat." It seemed Christmas was the hardest time of the year for Cat and her boys. She would watch as other families seemed to live in the land of MORE and she lived in the land of NOT ENOUGH. Rarely would there be any money left over to bless her guys with a few toys for Christmas.

CAT

Her two boys were all she had after a tragic divorce due to addiction.

However, one thing Cat had was a support system. She had people who would each take a portion of her boy's Christmas lists to ensure they had something under the tree.

She remained faithful at church. She struggled financially but as she began to understand there was an overflow in giving. Her life began to change. She decided she would tithe and honor the Lord with the first 10% of her income. Soon she found you can't outgive God. He always gives back more than you give. It's part of the law of the overflow.

You Can't Outgive God

God began speaking to Cat about helping others. In 2011 a young boy named David and his family were on the verge of being homeless. She knew he would not get a Christmas gift, and as she had received family help with her boys, she wanted to help him. He was between the ages of her own boys and her heart broke for David and his mom. Cat reached out on social media and she made an appeal. She asked if anybody could give a little extra to help David and his family. What many didn't realize was that she was facing her own financial nightmare. She barely had enough to cover her own needs. But she saw a way to let the overflow of her heart touch someone else. That's where real ministry begins. It was out of this struggle and pain a heart overflowing with love began to grow. A heart not focused on her own pain but on the pain of others.

Multiplication Started

Soon she started giving over and above her tithe. That's when God began to multiply her income. A blessing happened in her life. She received an inheritance. Instead of keeping it all for herself she gave part of the money to help someone adopt a child. Then she helped with another adoption and then another. It started to snowball and she soon found out that giving was a heart issue, not a *how much is in your bank account* issue. It was a decision that she had to make to become a person who would live in the overflow. It was a decision that would forever change her life. Even in her own need, she gave.

As time went on, her financial situation improved greatly. She didn't want to forget where she came from, and what the Lord had done, so she decided she would be the answer for other needy parents at Christmas.

"Give, and it will be given to you: good measure, pressed down, shaken together, and running over will be put into your bosom. For with the same measure that you use, it will be measured back to you." (Luke 6:38 NKJV)

Anchored In Giving

It's been seven years now that Catherine Garcia started Anchored In Giving (AIG). Her own charitable organization has now helped over 116 families at Christmas.

Each family receives a cash gift of at least $250 and multiple gifts as well. Usually Cat will schedule a meeting with the receiving family. Unaware of what is about to happen they meet at a location under the ruse that she wants to talk or hand them something. What she has planned is a big celebration. They will have no idea of what is about to happen. I've seen her meet people at Christmastime in the church parking lot. Tears streaming down from everyone's face receiving and especially from those giving. It's beautiful to watch a once defeated and desperate mother surprise a hurting family. She will take a few minutes and explain what she's been up to and then the packages start arriving. Each child will have a well-planned group of gifts.

There will be a few for the parents and then a cash gift for the extras they might need during Christmas. It is just amazing to watch. All from a once - single parent who knew what it was like to hurt. A parent who knew the hurt she had felt when knowing she didn't have anything to give her own boys. Many times the miracle of the overflow begins from a heart once filled with hurt, a heart that now overflows with love. Catherine Garcia has become a hurricane for Jesus!

Cat 5 For Jesus!

Cat ministering to a needy family. Thousands of gifts have been given by Anchored In Giving over the past seven years!

I've seen her meet people, at Christmastime in the church parking lot. Tears streaming down everyone's face receiving and especially on the faces of those giving.

Cat is quite the miracle. She loves unconditionally. She's a former single mom who was living day to day not really knowing how it would all work out but as she released herself to the Lord... what happened next has been amazing. As her pastor, I'm so proud of her.

One of Cat's Christmas wrapping parties. Her overflow of love is involving others in the overflow of giving! Giving is contagious at Crossroads!

One Boy Became Ten!

Two years ago, at Christmas, Cat was given a name of a needy boy. It was pretty late in the season and she was tapped out. She had given and given and touched many that Christmas. She pulled together a few really nice gifts and made her plan to stop by and visit the boy and drop off the gifts. When she showed up her heart sank. It wasn't the home of single boy it was the home of ten boys. It was a boy's home. She told me later how she wished she had known, she could have rallied some more people to help make it happen. She could see the disappointment in the faces of the other boys. She had nothing else. She promised that she would bring Christmas the next year to all the boys. And the next year she did. She pulled together the best Christmas those guys had ever seen.

And pure happiness filled the house!

That is living in the overflow. It's loving and living and giving yourself to others. It's becoming like Christ in caring and serving others. For Cat, it's the joy she feels when she makes others know they are loved. This young mom of two has become a special Santa to so many needy children. And she has involved dozens of our Crossroads family.

"Freely you have received, freely give."
(Matthew 10:8b NKJV)

Study Guide Chapter 2
Just Enough or More Than Enough
"Full of Nothing!"

Philippians 4:6 NKJV
"Be anxious for nothing, but in everything by prayer and supplication, with thanksgiving, let your requests be made known to God;"

Have you ever had just enough money to buy something? Perhaps you dropped into a convenience store to buy a coke and discovered you were short a nickel or a penny? Thankfully they have that little extra change dish. Some kind person left you a coin or two to help you out.

Write Something Good God Did for You This Week.

_____
_____
_____
_____
_____

Do You Know Someone Who Lives in the Overflow Who Doesn't Seem to Have a Lot?
Without mentioning their names to others can you share a little about what you've seen them do to help others?

_____
_____
_____
_____
_____

James 1:27 NKJV
"Pure and undefiled religion before God and the Father is this: to visit orphans and widows in their trouble, and to keep oneself unspotted from the world."

Who Do You Know that You Can Bring the Overflow to?

_____

_____

_____

_____

_____

_____

Luke 12:48 NKJV
"For everyone to whom much is given, from him much will be required; and to whom much has been committed, of him they will ask the more."

What if You Lived in the Overflow...
What Would That Look Like?

_____

_____

_____

_____

_____

Psalm 2:8 NKJV
"Ask of Me, and I will give You The nations for Your inheritance, And the ends of the earth for Your possession."

My son Michael and I heading home from Africa

Chapter 3

Let it Flow!
Be Generous with the Overflow!

"Give, and it will be given to you: good measure, pressed down, shaken together, and running over will be put into your bosom. For with the same measure that you use, it will be measured back to you."   (Luke 6:38 NKJV)

Generosity gives birth to generosity. Have you ever been in line at Christmastime, waiting for coffee or a hot latte, you get to the window to pay and the attendant says, "The person in front of you just paid for your drink." Immediately you feel this sense of wow! What a cool thing for someone to do. They don't know me. Some stranger just blessed me. Then you turn to the cashier and say, "Hey, I'll catch the car behind me." You have no idea who they are, and you generously pay for a cup of coffee because someone did it for you. Generosity gives birth to generosity.

Generosity is like a big rolling ball. If you can ever get it going, watch out because the momentum is amazing. You start giving and that giving will begin to give birth to more giving. You will discover great joy in giving.

Throughout my life I have found that to be true. But you have to want to give. You have to want to share. The overflow of generosity is not learned overnight. I've failed at this more than once, but for every time I've failed I've proven He blesses over and over a hundred times more by obeying His voice.

The hardest thing for anyone to deal with is their selfish heart. We're all selfish. We all want what is ours, and we want to keep it. We're all born like that. We are born with this sin nature that wants to keep and hoard what we have. We don't want to give it away. We want to take.

Mine!

It's the favorite word of every two-year-old, "MINE!" It comes so naturally to them. They are wired from the womb saying mine!

I don't remember where I found this list but it's entirely appropriate. It's called Toddler Property Laws:
1. If I like it, it's mine.
2. If I can take it away from you, it's mine.
3. If I had it a while ago, it's mine.
4. If I say it is mine, it's mine.
5. If it looks like mine it's mine.
6. If I say I saw it first, it's mine.
7. If you're having fun with it, it's mine.
8. If you lay it down, it's mine.
9. When I'm done with it, it's yours, until I want it back.
10. If it's broken, it's yours!

Many people are just like that with their money. It's mine! We are corrupt and full of our own self-interests. And our sin nature needs to change. We need to repent and become what Christ calls us to become.

David said, when he had sinned against God, "Create in me a clean heart, O God, and renew a right spirit within me." (Psalm 51:10 MEV)

We need a new heart. A clean, fresh heart. An unselfish heart. A heart that runs after God and wants to be generous like our heavenly Father. Think of how generous God has been with you. If He would be so generous with us why shouldn't we be generous with Him?

"God blesses you when you give with the right heart."
Robert Morris – Lead Pastor, Gateway Church

Too many times the problem is we want *to get* so we give with the wrong motive. *We give to get.* We will try tithing, if we get something immediately back. People give up too quickly because seeds are planted in their first tithe, but they never keep tithing to see the long-term benefit of tithing.

Make a Budget and Put God First

Danielle and I have been faithfully tithing for almost forty years. We have sheets of paper, from years of handmade monthly budgets. Stacks and stacks of notebook paper. That's what we started on way back when. At the beginning of every week we would calculate what we were going to make. And whatever the gross amount was we then divided by 10 and 1/10 or 10% was our tithe. We would then write a check for that amount. For years that was the way we did it. Now we give through the church app but it's the same idea. The first 10% of our gross income goes to our local church for the tithe. That's what tithe means: 10%.

Give to Get or Get to Give?

Another great principle to remember is *we get to give not give to get.* Here at Crossroads during a typical Sunday service, we will many times when we receive the tithe speak a tither's blessing. That blessing is really about you faithfully serving in generosity and giving to the Lord. It is a declaration from the pastor that implores God to bless these faithful people generously. To generously pour a blessing on them they can't even receive. Just like it says in Malachi 3 - open the windows of heaven over them.

See, I want you to experience the joy of giving. This is not a scheme. My desire for you to live in the overflow is not so you can spend more on yourselves, but so you can be a better steward and experience the overflow of God's blessings in your life. You will have greater finances and you will be blessed. But the blessing is so you can be a blessing.

I want each believer to experience the overflow. I want to be generous with my life. I want to be a generous husband, father, pastor and leader. I hope I never come across as stingy. Generosity should flow freely from all of us, especially if we proclaim Christ as Lord.

No one was more generous than Jesus. He gave His very life for the sin of the world. He willingly died for all of us. That is generosity to the utmost extent. Paul says it in Romans 5:8 MEV, "But God demonstrates His own love toward us, in that while we were yet sinners, Christ died for us." He loved us! That's more than generous - that's insane. That's a level of love and sacrifice I have a hard time understanding, but that's what He did for all of us.

Faith Gives Birth to Generosity

My good friend Gary Sapp often says, "God will get it to you if He can get it through you." God wants to give generously to us but too many times instead of being a conduit of His generosity we are a stopping point. He wants us to release faith so that generosity can happen. Generosity happens when you have a heart that is full of faith.

"And without faith it is impossible to please God, for he who comes to God must believe that He exists and that He is a rewarder of those who diligently seek Him."
(Hebrews 11:6 MEV)

Faith gives birth to generosity. If you'll release faith, you can discover generosity. You'll stop giving out of what you have left over to what is obedience to the Holy Spirit. The Holy Spirit will teach you about giving. I can't tell you how many times I've felt the Holy Spirit's prompting me to give to someone. So, I reach into my wallet to give and within minutes I've had a blessing already back in my hand from somewhere else because I was faithful to listen to what the Holy Spirit was telling me to do.

Instead of a selfish heart, ask God to develop a generous heart within you. A heart that overflows with Christ's love. Not just for the random need but for the daily need that comes knocking all the time. Ask Him to help you be ready to touch someone today.

Tithes

Remember, generosity gives birth to generosity. Jacob and Monica Sosa are a young couple in our church. They have a trucking business. A few years ago, Jacob started attending my early prayer time. He was frustrated. He had more bills than money. I challenged him to start tithing. I said, "Jacob if you'll tithe for 90 days I know God will show you He is real, and His way of blessing is real." I said, "If He doesn't prove to you in 90 days that He can meet your need, then I'll reimburse you 100% what you paid to the church." He looked shocked. Jacob and Monica began to tithe. Guess what happened? Their business turned around.

Please understand a tithe is 10% of your income. Not a tip of 1 or 2%.

Jacob now has four trucks running and his business is booming. He is a faithful tither. He just asked me the other day to pray with him that he could find some property because his business is growing so much. That is the result of a heart that is generous and living in the overflow.

People who love to give have developed a grateful heart. They are grateful for all God has done in their lives. They remember what they once were and how they were lost in sin. They remember what sin did to them and how desperate they were to find life and build a new future. This grateful heart develops because they start obeying God's word and they see God is not a mean, lightning-bolt-throwing deity, but He is a loving Father who desires to bless His people.

The Test

Malachi the prophet dealt with the children of Israel. He spoke to their rebellion. They had rebelled against God in NOT paying their tithe. See I believe you pay a tithe and you give an offering. The tithe is Holy, so it BELONGS to the Lord. It's already His. I'm just returning to Him what is rightfully His. By doing that He then blesses my life. Malachi delivers this powerful rebuke to Israel:

[8] "Will a man rob God? Yet you have robbed Me. But you say, "How have we robbed You?" In tithes and offerings. [9] You are cursed with a curse, your whole nation, for you are robbing Me. [10] Bring all the tithes into the storehouse, that there may be food in My house, and test Me now in this, says the Lord of Hosts, if I will not open for you the windows of heaven and

pour out for you a blessing, that *there will* not *be room* enough *to receive it.* [11] I will rebuke the devourer for your sakes, so that it will not destroy the fruit of your ground, and the vines in your field will not fail to bear fruit, says the Lord of Hosts. [12] Then all the nations will call you blessed, for you will be a delightful land, says the Lord of Hosts." (Malachi 3:8-12 MEV)

I believe in this Scripture so much! We have it posted just inside the entrance of our sanctuary, where we have drop boxes for offerings, because we want our people blessed. Of course, this is just one of the ways you can give financially at Crossroads. I want them to remember to keep the Lord first. To bring ALL the tithes into the storehouse. We're not to give our tithe to the TV evangelist or a local charity or the United Way. It belongs in the house of the Lord. It belongs in the church you attend and where you are fed weekly.

This is the TEST God gives to all believers. He says, "...test Me now in this." We are testing God to see if He will and He is testing us to see if we will.

Windows of Heaven Open

"... if I will not open for you the windows of heaven and pour out for you a blessing, that *there will* not *be room* enough *to receive it.*"

That sounds like the kind of OVERFLOW I'd like to get in front of. What if God poured so much on you, you couldn't contain it? When you start allowing God to bless you in the overflow you will experience times of testing where it seems you are waiting, but your trusting God will come through. You'll find out like Jacob and Monica did. *You can't outgive God!*

Then He says in verse 11,

"I will rebuke the devourer for your sakes, so that it will not destroy the fruit of your ground, and the vines in your field will not fail to bear fruit, says the Lord of Hosts."
(Malachi 3:11 MEV)

So many people have everything devoured every month. Before they can spend it, something happens and the devourer destroys it. It's eaten up by car trouble, home repairs, sickness, and difficulties of all types. But imagine God standing there saying, "No, not this home; this home is in covenant with me and I am going to bless this home. They are trusting me, and they have set this as a test for me and I am going to prove to them, that I am a God who cannot lie."

"In hope of eternal life which God, who cannot lie, promised before the world began." (Titus 1:2 MEV)

What an incredible challenge the God of the universe gives to us. He says, "Test me!"

Just as God says TEST Me, I believe we also are tested. Every time we are paid we go through a test. It's the test of a good steward. I'm tested in being faithful to that same covenant. If I believe *He is able to be tested and not afraid of that* then why wouldn't I say alrighty - I will follow through on my part? Test me and see if I will be faithful also. I've taken that test over and over in my life. Week after week Nellie and I have been consistent to give our tithe and offering to the Lord. People wonder why we are so blessed. It's the blessing of the overflow from being faithful with what God has given us.

Extravagant Giving

Years ago, we were building a family life center at the church. I made a commitment that Danielle and I would be a part of

74

that fundraising effort. We didn't make a lot of money. I think at that time our annual income was around $18,000 a year. She didn't work outside the home so that was our total income. I felt the Lord wanted us to give $1,000. We didn't have it to give.

We were already paying our tithe, and giving to missions, and now we felt God was telling us we needed to give something special, above all the rest. For us this was a great sacrifice, but how could we? We lived in a rent house and barely made ends meet every month. We literally would have $20-30 dollars a week left over after all our bills were paid. I had to do odd jobs for us to even make it! But I knew God was speaking to me.

It was like the Old Testament story of the widow and the prophet. In 2 Kings 4, the prophet Elisha comes to her and asks what's in her house? All she had was a jar of oil. If we had a jar of oil it was not very full, but don't get me wrong - we were happy, and it always seemed we made it. We didn't have tons of anything, but we had each other, and a baby boy and we were living in the overflow. *At least we had faith like we lived in the overflow.* We knew it was a miracle God had placed us in such a wonderful church and we were so grateful. How could we not give?

I started looking for anything I could sell to raise the money. I tried thinking of odd jobs I could do extra over the extra side jobs I was already doing. Finally, the only thing of value we had at the time was our car, an Oldsmobile Cutlass and it had some equity in it. I took out a $1,000 loan on that Cutlass, and that's how we gave that overflow gift.

I've tried remembering how that all ended up. Did we get a miracle payback? Did someone hand me $1,000 and we were so thankful we stepped out in faith? I think we just gave it and paid the note until it was paid off. As I recall nothing spectacular at the time happened other than we got to be a part of the future of all those kids. That expansion was for the future. We didn't give to get. We gave it to sow into the lives of the next generation. It was a massive amount to us. We didn't have it, but we were so happy when we wrote that check. We had been obedient to what the Holy Spirit had urged us to give. And that's exactly how you will feel when you obey His prompting also.

"Give, and it will be given to you: good measure, pressed down, shaken together, and running over will be put into your bosom. For with the same measure that you use, it will be measured back to you."   (Luke 6:38 NKJV)

So, if you give with teaspoon faith I guess you'll get a teaspoon of overflow back into your life. If you give shovels you'll receive shovels of blessing. But what if you gave dump truck loads? The generosity law states you're going to get back dump truck loads of blessings. The fun begins when you start telling yourself, "Well I need to see how much I can give and see if God will match that?" This could get crazy fun. Just being an instrument of faith in His hands. Challenge yourself in saying, "God I want to be used in the overflow of generosity."

Sacrifice

Today, I look around and I remember that time in my life. I think how much of a sacrifice it was, and how God has blessed Danielle and me and our family over and over again. People look at us and think wow, they never run short, they never have struggles. We have been tested for 40 years on giving and are tested every day, just like everyone else, but we've learned when the Spirit speaks we need to be available to give and be what He's called us to be. Sacrifice is usually never easy. That is why it's called sacrifice. There's the setting aside of a want or genuine need to make it happen. Maybe we postpone something we were going to do. It would probably be safe to say that, Dave Ramsey would not suggest you take out a loan to give and I'm not suggesting you do that either. That was what we did. We wanted to be a part in a significant way and it was right for us.

When I think of sacrifice and extravagance I think of how much God loved me. He sacrificed His one and only Son on the cross. He literally gave His best. He gave extravagantly so I could have eternal life. He followed through with a divine plan to save me. How could I not try and do my best? I want to be a part of the plan to win all of mankind.

When God spoke to Abraham to offer Isaac it seemed the most bizarre request. This boy was the promised future of the line of the house of Abraham. It would be through Abraham's Isaac that all the nations of the earth would be blessed. Why does God now ask Abraham to sacrifice this child? Even young Isaac was curious to what his dad was up to when they walked up the steep hill of Mount Moriah.

"Abraham said, "My son, God will provide for Himself the lamb for a burnt offering." So, the two of them went together.[9] Then they came to the place that God had told him. So, Abraham built an altar there and arranged the wood; and he bound Isaac his son and laid him on the altar, on the wood. [10] Then Abraham stretched out his hand and took the knife to slay his son. [11] But the angel of the Lord called to him out of heaven and said, "Abraham, Abraham!"

And he said, "Here I am."

¹² Then He said, "Do not lay your hands on the boy or do anything to him, because now I know that you fear God, seeing you have not withheld your only son from Me." ¹³ Then Abraham lifted up his eyes and looked, and behind him was a ram caught in a thicket by his horns. So, Abraham went and took the ram and offered him up as a burnt offering in the place of his son. ¹⁴ Abraham <u>called the name of that place The Lord Will Provide,</u> as it is said to this day, "In the mount of the Lord it will be provided." ¹⁵ Then the angel of the Lord called to Abraham out of heaven a second time, ¹⁶ and said, "By Myself I have sworn, says the Lord, because you have done this thing, and have not withheld your son, your only son, ¹⁷ I will indeed bless you and I will indeed multiply your descendants as the stars of the heavens and as the sand that is on the seashore. Your descendants will possess the gate of their enemies. ¹⁸ Through your offspring all the nations of the earth will be blessed, because you have obeyed My voice." (Genesis 22:8-18 MEV)

God saw the faith of Abraham. He could see he truly believed Him and whatever He asks Abraham to do, he would do it. He is unwavering. He is obedient to what God has requested. And because Abraham doesn't waver God puts a special blessing on him. He will be blessed, and all his descendants will multiply, and they will possess the gates of their enemies.

What does Abraham do?

He worships in the overflow of his heart and names the place Jehovah-jireh, meaning the Lord will provide. Abraham would have never experienced the Lord Jehovah-jireh if he hadn't obeyed God. There's a whole new lesson to be learned when you are obedient. There is the refreshing of remembering who God was to you during that season.

Kevin Fisher, a member of my board of advisors, is a giver. I've known him for thirty years. He is a petrophysicist. On the occasion of his twenty-year anniversary at Schlumberger, the company gave him a Rolex watch. That's a pretty nice gift and one you really want to cherish.

Almost every summer for the past thirteen years he has taken his family on a mission trip to Kenya. They sponsor children at our schools and have also built many churches and worked on various projects through our church. They always sign up and take their vacation to help.

A few years ago, they signed up as usual but had no one to sit and watch their dogs while they were away. The entire family of 5 took the trip while dog watchers were at the house. The dog watchers invited some people over to the Fisher's home and unfortunately the Rolex was stolen.

When Kevin and his family returned there were of course some upset feelings. It was a real loss of a wonderful keepsake. Nothing ever happened to the people who took the watch, and the story was a bitter pill to swallow. A few years later a phone call came, and a man with a foreign accent was on the other end of the line. He asked Kevin if he was Kevin Fisher who had worked at Schlumberger? He said he was, and the unknown caller said,

"I have your watch."

It had been three years. The police had no leads. It was a non-issue now. It was over. Close the book. He lost an expensive watch. Was this a scam? Was this for real? Kevin knew he would never see the watch again. Kevin then agreed to meet the man and he said, "I bought the watch for $1,000 and want to return it to you." Kevin was so thankful. He offered to pay the man back the $1,000 and the man declined. He said, "I cannot, I must do this. I will not let you repay me."

When I think of tithing, I think how God can cause someone to return to you what had been stolen. He rewards you when you are faithful and extravagant in your giving. You give not just a tithe, but you give over and beyond. That is giving with a generous heart. That is giving in the overflow. That is the kind of giving that will prompt God to not only rebuke a devourer, but he will have a Rolex returned to you. And you don't even have to pay it back.

You want to live in the overflow with your finances?

Start paying the tithe that belongs to the Lord! Start setting aside that first 10% and watch the windows of heaven start to open.

You want to see God bless you even more?

Start giving extravagantly from the overflow of your heart! Watch out! There will be more than you can receive coming your way. "Try me," says the Lord. You will not be disappointed. I've experienced it over and over. Others have reaped the blessing of obedience. Put God to the test. He tells you it's okay. Put the challenge out there to Him. *God I will test you in this because that's what your word says.* Now as I exercise faith, you release your blessings over my life.

Faith, Generosity, Overflow, Blessing

In its simplest form this is what I've experienced, and this is what I believe. You've got to have FAITH in God, through Jesus Christ, to experience living in the overflow! That's where it all begins. You exercise your faith to believe He is. You believe that God is able. It's not faith in a system but faith in God. Faith moves mountains. Faith conquers the NO that wants to live in your heart every day. Faith destroys doubt. Faith says "YES!" Faith in God's word and His promises will give birth to generosity.

Generosity that has been birthed out of faith in Christ says, "God has blessed me so much and I've just got to do this." As faith grows and generosity is given a heart to grow in, then generosity looks for opportunity. A genuine love for others will grow. As that love develops and selfishness is defeated, generosity will no longer feel like it has to judge the reason I give. Or is that person worthy of my generosity? Generosity remembers where it came from and resists fear. Because fear will always tell you that you don't have enough. Fear will paralyze the faith that's trying to grow in your heart. Generosity is your heart. Generosity is your passion. I give what's in my heart. I'm generous because of the journey I've had up to now. I realize my journey from here forward is going to be greater if I am generous with what God has given me.

Out of this generosity begins to emerge this heart of overflow. When I allow the generosity to flow there will soon become an overflow of His blessing in my life. Overflow is the fruit of faith and generosity when I follow what God is speaking to me. And when I allow faith to be released, watch out because overflow is about to happen. Overflow will give birth to blessing. Blessing will pour on my life. It will pour over onto my family. It will pour onto my friends, co-workers, and blessing will pour onto the next generation after me.

I'm reaping today from generations before me who decided to follow Christ. Their decisions to serve the Lord still overflow my journey. How can I not let faith grow and become generosity? Generosity from faith in Christ is not pity! It is a heart of compassion for the wounded and dying in this life. I want them to experience the same generosity of God's love that I have received, whether it's the generosity of a dollar or the generosity of me stopping to lend a hand. That generosity will cause overflow to happen in my life. I will experience overflow as a fruit of my heart filled with faith in God and the release of His generous love growing through me.

One day I will enjoy the ultimate overflow of my faith in God. The overflow of heaven. We believers will be the recipients of all the things that Christ has prepared for us that love Him. We will reap the blessings of lives lived in the overflow of God's love.

Be Generous with what God has Given to You!

Study Guide Chapter 3

Let it Flow!

Be Generous with the Overflow!

Luke 6:38 NKJV

"Give, and it will be given to you: good measure, pressed down, shaken together, and running over will be put into your bosom. For with the same measure that you use, it will be measured back to you."

Generosity gives birth to generosity. Have you ever been in line at Christmastime, waiting for coffee or a hot latte, you get to the window to pay and the attendant says, "The person in front of you just paid for your drink." Immediately you feel this sense of wow! What a cool thing for someone to do. They don't know me. Some stranger just blessed me. Then you turn to the cashier and say, "Hey, I'll catch the car behind me." You have no idea who they are, and you generously pay for a cup of coffee because someone did it for you. Generosity gives birth to generosity.

Describe the Difference Between Give to Get and Get to Give

_____
_____
_____
_____
_____

Hebrews 11:6 MEV

"And without faith it is impossible to please God, for he who comes to God must believe that He exists and that He is a rewarder of those who diligently seek Him."

Why Do You Need to Have Faith to Be Generous?

_____
_____
_____
_____

What Percentage of Your Income is a Tithe?

_____ 1% _____3% _____7%_____10% _____100%

Who Are We Testing When We Pay Tithe?

_____
_____
_____
_____

What Does Generosity Give Birth to?

_____

How Often Should We Pay Tithe?

_____
_____
_____
_____

What is the Name Abraham Gives to God at Mt. Moriah?

_____
_____
_____

What Does Jehovah-jireh Mean?

_____
_____
_____

If God Met Abraham's Need, Can He Meet Your Need?

_____Yes _____No

Isaiah 54:17 NKJV
"No weapon formed against you shall prosper, and every tongue which rises against you in judgment You shall condemn. This is the heritage of the servants of the Lord, and their righteousness is from Me," Says the Lord."

My daughter Lacey and I at the Mara River in Kenya

Chapter 4

Praying in the Overflow

"If we are going to RECEIVE the OVERFLOW, we must pray in the OVERFLOW!"

Prayer has been the catalyst for change in my life. No one can reach the throne of heaven without prayer.

"But seek first the kingdom of God and His righteousness, and all these things will be added to you." (Matthew 6:33 ESV)

A Familiar Path

Lou made her way to the barn, walking down the familiar path. She was warming her hands by taking turns with one hand in a pocket, and then the other, exchanging it with the cold handle of the milk can. The first rays of light were just beginning to break through the thick dark clouds. Her dress was wet from the dew covering the ground, rubbing against its edges. A line of golden light rays peeked delicately through the darkness revealing the coming sunrise. And a mist covered the pond whose surface was interrupted with an occasional splash of a bass, sounding from its waters.

It was a beautiful morning. Each sight and sound reminded her of her childhood. She was born during the Civil War, her childhood was hard, and the family always lived under the strain of not enough. The war had taken a lot from her family. It had destroyed many farms, towns and cities. The country had been devastated. Over 600,000 lives were lost in the War between the States. The beautiful Georgia she once knew was in shambles and would be for years to come.

Gen William Tecumseh Sherman   Gen John Corse

"On November 10, 1864, the Union General William Tecumseh Sherman issued orders from a home in downtown Rome, Georgia, to General John Corse. Gen. Sherman said, "Tonight destroy all public property not needed by your command, all foundries, mills, workshops, warehouses, railroad depots, or other storehouses convenient to the railroad, together with all wagon shops, tanneries or other factories useful to the enemy. Destroy all bridges immediately, then move your command to Kingston." footnote https://romegeorgia.org/civil-war/history/

Rome was burned that night, thus marking the beginning of Sherman's March to the Sea. Four days later, there in Rome, Georgia, on November 14, a beautiful, healthy little girl was born to Nimrod and Catherine Huggins. They named her Lucinda Catherine.

This little girl would grow up to become a no-nonsense woman. Maybe it was because life had been hard growing up during and after the Civil War. It must have been very difficult rebuilding everything. Maybe that was part of the reason her family eventually moved to Blount County, Alabama. Nothing would be the same after the War between the States, not for a long, long time. But at least they had their family.

As little Lucy grew up she learned that everyone worked on the farm. Young and old, you had a chore or something that you were supposed to do. It was a working farm and the family depended on you to get your job done! Later, when her siblings would be born she would help momma and papa teach the others to work too. Everybody did their part.

As she got older, her serious nature was well-balanced with a deep, abiding love for the Lord. Mixed in with a hard work ethic, she became a woman who enjoyed her early morning times with her Savior. Her Methodist upbringing had taught her to love the Bible and prayer. She took advantage of those moments in the barn and prayed while she milked the cows.

Love and Loss

In 1883 Lou fell in love with a handsome young man. At nineteen, she and her beau, Houston Cornelius, were married. Their families lived in Dry Creek Settlement, Blount County, Alabama, and Houston and Lou were blessed with two sweet little girls, Emma and Minnie. Life was great, and it seemed set, until tragedy struck their little family. Just three years into this perfect love story, Houston was struck down with typhoid fever and left Lucinda a widow at twenty-two. It would be five years before she would find love again and marry Houston's second cousin Raymond. At twenty-seven, and with two kids in tow, she and Raymond were to be married. He had spoken to Mr. Huggins and was given permission to marry his widowed daughter. The day he came to fetch her, they would have to travel to where the minister was. The preacher was a circuit-rider-preacher and had to be found. In those days, there weren't enough preachers and many communities didn't have a church house but a school or a saloon that would function as a church on the day the preacher showed up.

Whenever he came to town, that's when the saints would gather. Many preachers rotated through a different town each Sunday of any given month. Someone had said they thought he was a few towns over.

January 1891

It was a cold January morning in 1891 when Raymond came-a-calling. He spoke to Mr. Huggins, Lou's daddy, asked if he could take her as his wife. Mr. Huggins, blessed them and said, "when they returned that they would have a great time celebrating their wedding day." Take care of my Lucy girl and we'll see yawl when yawl get back," he said. He and momma Huggins would take care of Emma and Minnie until they returned.

Ray had an old wooden buckboard and he and Lou set out to find the preacher. He whistled to that old mule and called to walk steady, "gitty-up!" He hummed a simple tune. Both Ray and Lou were nervous and yet anticipated a great new life together. On the way, as the buckboard rocked back and forth, he looked over to Lou and gently reached over to hold her hand. With a determined look and a firm pulling away, she told her soon-to-be husband, "There will be none of that sir, until the preacher says his words over us!" Raymond smiled and went back to calling to the mules. "Alrighty Lucinda, alrighty, soon enough, soon enough I reckon." That evening, still not finding the preacher, they built a fire, and Lou cooked a meal. After supper they laid on their bedrolls under the stars. It was a perfect time for the conversation to be of their hopes and dreams and of their life together.

I can only imagine how amazing it was to travel off together in one direction, both single and searching for the preacher, and returning married, and ready for the next great chapter in their lives.

Raymond and Lucinda Cornelius

Lucy had two little girls that needed a daddy. She was young and strong and had a strikingly beautiful presence. Most men didn't want a woman with children. But Raymond loved Lucinda Catherine. He had seen her several times and when he heard about Houston's death, he felt bad for the young mom and prayed for an opportunity to meet her. When he finally got his introduction, he fell in love with her almost immediately. She was a lot slower to convince but it made sense and the girls needed a hardworking father. He wasn't Houston, but he had other qualities that made her attracted to him. She liked his broad shoulders. "He looks like a worker!" she said. And of course, she liked his curly hair. But most of all, it was important to her that his last name was Cornelius and that the girls would have the same last name. Eventually, they found that preacher and the knot was tied. And of course, there was no touching, kissing or even holding of hands until the final amen. Eventually she and Raymond would have three more beautiful little girls: Mittie, Myla and Ruth.

An Unusual Sanctuary

Opening the barn each morning became a wonderful ritual for Lucinda. The smell of the hay and feed, the rooster crowing as morning broke. She enjoyed being a wife and a momma of five girls. She loved life, and hardships seemed distant at the moment. Raymond had been a good husband and their simple life on the farm was pleasant. Even though she enjoyed their life, she also found that even Christians experience trials and difficulties. Periodically her and Ray would find themselves in a test or going through one of those difficulties.

Lou had found the early hours of the day were the perfect time to pray. Her and her Lord would meet every morning, just before sunrise. Out at the barn, she'd gather her little stool and move it over near Sally, that ole jersey milk cow. She warmed her hands and placed the bucket into position. Sally could produce quite an abundance of milk. The family always enjoyed the early morning blessing of her bounty. As Lucy began to fill the bucket with Sally's milk, she would pray. She prayed and prayed. It was only Lucy and that cow in the sanctuary of that barn. With her voice filling the rafters with songs of praise and prayers pouring forth, Lucy lifted her attention heavenward.

"Blessed are those who hunger and thirst for righteousness, for they shall be filled." (Matthew 5:6 NKJV)

"But seek first the kingdom of God and his righteousness, and all these things will be added to you. 34 "Therefore do not be anxious about tomorrow, for tomorrow will be anxious for itself. Sufficient for the day is its own trouble."
(Matthew 6:33-34 ESV)

"Lord, if that's You, do it Again!"

But on this morning, something strange began to happen as she prayed. As she got lost in her time of prayer and lifting up the name of the Lord, and celebrating His greatness, she started to feel something different as she spoke. She felt the glory of the Lord filling her heart. It was like electricity coursing up and down her spine. A strange thick feeling and tingling in her tongue came upon her. Unintelligible words were filling her mind. She kept trying to press through it and then all of a sudden, a different and a powerful language came from her voice. Nothing like this had ever happened to this staunch Methodist. She stopped. She turned her head to see if anyone was in the barn with her. What was that? What is going on, she thought? The feeling kept intensifying. She began to pray again and with more fervency she lifted the name of the Lord in praise. Again, she felt a glorious power coming over her words, and what sounded like a foreign language was pouring out of her. Her tongue felt amazing and wonderful, and a powerful something was happening to her.

She stopped and asked, "Lord is that you?" She waited. Then she said, *"Lord, if that's you, do it again!"* And immediately she began to praise the name of Jesus in the most amazing heavenly language. It erupted out of her heart in a glorious shout of victory. It flowed like a river. The blessed baptism of the Holy Spirit was released, and what followed would forever change her life and generations to come. She spoke in this unknown tongue for quite a while. The cow was her only companion and partner in this early visitation. Lou was lost in the presence of her Savior.

Enjoy the Overflow!

She laughed and sang through the morning. She prayed for distant fields of ministry and that this same blessing would fall on all. The chores would be delayed today, if they happened at all. Lou lost all presence of time and place. She and her wonderful Savior were having a communion of heavenly proportions.

Finally, she settled down and sat there in holy wonder. Wiping tears of joy from her eyes she began to ask herself, "What was this? What had happened?" Is this what they said occurred in the book of Acts when they spoke, in an unknown tongue, and received the baptism of the Holy Spirit? Is this that baptism of fire Jesus spoke about? Surely it is! **It is!** She had just been filled with God's Holy Spirit with the evidence of speaking in an unknown tongue!

After a while, she remembered Raymond would be wondering where she was. It was strange he and the girls hadn't come to look for her but as she got up to run to tell him the great news, he came into the barn. Throughout the morning she told him all that had happened. She felt like heaven had fallen into that little barn, and that it had been transformed into the grandest cathedral. She remembered a quote from the book of Acts that was a fulfillment of the prophet Joel.

"But this is that which was spoken by the prophet Joel; 17 And it shall come to pass in the last days, saith God, I will pour out of my Spirit upon all flesh: and your sons and your daughters shall prophesy, and your young men shall see visions, and your old men shall dream dreams: 18 And on my servants and on my hand maidens I will pour out in those days of my Spirit; and they shall prophesy:" (Acts 2:16-18 KJV)

Lou was my great grandmother, Lucinda Catherine Cornelius. She was my mom's grandmother. Her mother's mother that I never met. She went to heaven the year before I was born. I remember growing up and hearing these stories. I heard how she was an amazing woman of God about the powerful baptism in the Holy Spirit she experienced, in that barn in Poarch, Oklahoma.

I too have discovered the value of early morning prayer. I have found that seeking the Lord every morning has become the game changer for life and ministry. It is the fuel to my day. It's finding the overflow of His holy presence. The Holy Spirit is the force behind God moving in my life. It is in and through Him that I am able to minister. It's the same overflow that Lucinda Cornelius had. Thank you Lord for giving it to me also.

Grandma and the Overflow

"Grandma" as Momma called her, was a mighty woman of God. She found out that the Lord had MORE for her! He wanted to pour out MORE on her and everyone else.

It was always there. It was like an unopened gift. Strange, she hadn't seen it or used it or even asked to receive it. It just happened one morning while milking a cow. Her praise for her Lord and her consistent prayer life had ushered her into the presence of the Lord's power! That MORE that God had for her forever changed her life.

She and Grandpa Cornelius left Oklahoma and went into the ministry shortly thereafter. She had gone to the old church that her entire family attended. She couldn't help but tell them what the Lord had done, and how He had filled her with His heavenly presence. You can't keep something like this a secret. This is too amazing! Everyone needs to receive this blessing!

Unfortunately, it was not received. The stern rebuke she received from the pastor, and the looks of wagging churchgoers heads, was an unexpected reception. She was promptly invited to leave. Well, that was alright with her, because the experience of Pentecost forever changed her life. It wouldn't be the first time someone didn't want the blessing, but what she received was MORE than she could have imagined.

I'm so thankful she was open to the MORE the Lord had for her. It was out of this MORE that she would minister for the next fifty years.

Raymond and Lucinda Cornelius,
Home Missionaries with
the Assemblies of God in 1917

She stopped and asked, "Lord is that you?" She waited... Then she said, "Lord, if that's you, do it again!"

Stepping Out in the Overflow

On October 29, 1910, she and Grandpa left Oklahoma and went out ordained as Home Missionaries by F. (Felix) A. Hale. Then later, on January 23, 1917, she requested and received credentials as a Home Missionary from the recently organized Assemblies of God. She and Grandpa pioneered churches in Electra, Plainview, Corsicana, Borger, Dodd's Corner, Vernon, Texas; and Portales, New Mexico. She preached all through the Texas panhandle, New Mexico, North Texas and Oklahoma. She held revivals and tent meetings, brush arbors, street meetings and was known as a woman of the word and of prayer. On one occasion, the family was run out of Lawton, Oklahoma, with rotten vegetables and spoiled fruit thrown in their faces, because of the gospel message. Persecution would not stop her determination to tell others about Jesus, or the power that He had given her. Grandma didn't let that bother her. Her calling was for a lifetime. One thing was for sure: a mighty anointing and holy resolve rested on her.

Momma told me more than once that Grandma was a serious woman, that she didn't have much use for frivolity and joking around! Her life was filled with prayer and the Bible.

Miracles Happen in the Overflow

Years into her ministry, a man in the town they lived in had been hit by a train. His injury was so bad that he died. They called for "Mother Cornelius" to come and pray for the man. The same power that flowed through Christ at His resurrection flowed through that amazing woman of God, and life came back into that man. Miracles, healings, hardships, persecutions, trials and blessings all came through this dedicated minister of the gospel.

My great grandmother, Lucinda Catherine Cornelius

Holy Desire for More

All because she wanted MORE! And she found MORE! When I hear of her life and testimony it causes me to want MORE!

More of You, Lord! I want MORE of Your power! MORE of Your love! MORE of Your anointing! MORE of Your victory, in my life! MORE of all You have for me!

If you want MORE, you'll have to spend MORE time in prayer. It won't happen through casual, unfocused prayer times, but it will come through a hunger and a thirst for MORE of the OVERFLOW!

Leonard Ravenhill once said, *"Little prayer little power, much prayer much power!"*

When will we learn that through hours on our knees the minutes we preach and minister will have greater effect?

"Not by might nor by power, but by My Spirit,' says the Lord of hosts." (Zechariah 4:6b NKJV)

We will not alter nations and change continents for Christ by casually approaching the throne of grace. We must worship in His holy presence with hearts ready to commune and spend unmeasured time at His feet. We must push back man-made agendas and schedules. We must make the move of His Spirit in our lives the greatest priority. We need hearts filled with desire and dedication. Heavenly Father fill us with holy anticipation. Fill us with holy desire to stay with you in unrestricted hours of devotion and prayer! Let us linger in your holy flow of anointing and power. Fill us with a greater measure of love for the lost. Help us to burn for souls to be saved and find that life in you.

Touch my lips with MORE!

Isaiah the prophet cries in hunger and desperation, "... And I said, Woe is me! For I am lost; for I am a man of unclean lips, and I dwell in the midst of a people of unclean lips; for my eyes have seen the King, the Lord of hosts!" 6 Then one of the seraphim flew to me, having in his hand a burning coal that he had taken with tongs from the altar. 7 And he touched my mouth and said: "Behold, this has touched your lips; your guilt is taken away, and your sin atoned for."   (Isaiah 6:5-7 ESV)

Oh, heavenly Father touch my lips! Touch my heart and make it clean! Hear us and heal us. Renew your right spirit within us so that we can receive all that you have.

A New Season of MORE!

It will be in seasons of connecting with our Heavenly Father. It will come when we have changed our simple surroundings into a house of prayer. It will flow out of rivers of tears of joy and worship as we bask in the magnitude of His greatness. A new season of MORE will come when the barns of our lives are changed, and they become places of worship and praise. I long for the place at your feet and hearing the gentle tones of your words. "Come to Me, all *you* who labor and are heavy laden, and I will give you rest."   (Matthew 11:28 NKJV

Will Reagan and the United Pursuit Band sing a song:
Set a fire down inside my soul. There's a lyric I love...

"Set a fire down in my soul that I can't contain that I can't control I want more of you God, I want more of you God Set a fire down in my soul that I can't contain that I can't control I want more of you God..."

Set a fire down in our souls and let it overflow!

"A new season of MORE will come when the barns of our lives are changed, and they become places of worship and praise."

Study Guide Questions for Chapter 4
Praying in the Overflow
"If we are going to pray in the OVERFLOW, we must pray in the OVERFLOW!"

Prayer has been the catalyst for change in my life. No one can reach the throne of heaven without prayer.

Matthew 6:33 ESV
"But seek first the kingdom of God and His righteousness, and all these things will be added to you."

Do You Have a Frequent Path You Take to Prayer?
If so describe it in a few sentences... (i.e., time, place and how often?)

_____
_____
_____
_____
_____

Describe an Overflow of His Presence Moment You've Experienced? (A powerful time of prayer)

_____
_____
_____
_____
_____

Matthew 5:6 NKJV
"Blessed are those who hunger and thirst for righteousness, for they shall be filled."

Leonard Ravenhill once said,
"Little prayer little power, much prayer much power!"

Any Old Areas (Barns) in Your Life That Need to Become Sanctuaries?

A new place you are using to seek God, driving to work, praying before bedtime, early somewhere special...etc.

_____
_____
_____
_____
_____
_____

Have You Been Used to Step Out in the Overflow to Touch Someone's Life?

Witness, pray for, give, encourage... etc.

_____
_____
_____
_____
_____

Zechariah 4:6 NKJV
"Not by might nor by power, but by My Spirit,' says the Lord of hosts."

If God Were to Give You a <u>NEW SEASON</u> of <u>MORE</u>, What Would You Hope it Would Bring About?

_____
_____
_____
_____
_____

Have You Experienced Miracles in the Overflow?

_____
_____
_____
_____
_____

Psalm 100:4 ESV
*"Enter His gates with thanksgiving, and His courts with praise!
Give thanks to Him; bless His name!"*

The front entrance of Crossroads Fellowship, Houston, Texas

Chapter 5

Worship in the Overflow

Let WORSHIP flow from the
OVERFLOW of the HOLY SPIRIT!

Worshiping in the OVERFLOW doesn't just happen. If we truly desire the overflow of God's presence, we must allow the overflow of worship to flow out of our hearts.

"Worship the Lord in the splendor of holiness;"
(Psalm 96:9a ESV)

It was 2012. My father - in - law, Dan Heil, invited my brother in-law John and me to take a trip to the Holy Land. I had been several times before, but this would be a different kind of trip. This would be our "do-it-yourself tour." We would seek out the unexpected and non-traditional sights. The "what did we miss before" places? It would be a pilgrimage of our own making. Not one of those pre-packaged and very well-organized Israel tours. We would go and make it up as we went.

I booked the flights and made the hotel arrangements. In Jerusalem, I chose a hotel, in the downtown area near Ben-Yehuda Street. Ben-Yehuda pedestrian mall in central Jerusalem is one of those Israel destinations that won't blow you away with its beauty or antiquity, but is one of those tourist attractions where you'll probably end up window shopping and drinking some really great coffee.

With our hotel nearby, several nights we took off in search of something three Americans would like to eat. I'm not very picky when dining out. I've often said, "I'm a lot like Will Rogers. When it comes to food, I've never met a plate of food I didn't like." However, my father-in-law is not cut from the same cloth. He's rather persnickety and John would want to dissect the conversation and diagram all the eating establishments before we leave.

An Interesting Night

Eventually we ended up at this really great restaurant with a wrought iron fish at its entrance. It was nicely lit and gave an air of "this might be a little pricey, but I bet it's going to be a delicious experience." They had inside and outside dining. The street - side dining was wonderful. The night was cool, and we were greeted by a comfortable breeze. We sat out under the night sky to have our meal.

I wish I could remember the name of that place. There are a lot of details I missed that evening but what I do remember is the incredible service we received. You've probably had that same experience. You went to a restaurant and a certain server was just extra special. Like they could read your mind.

A Terrible Experience

I preface this story by telling you what happened the night before. We had been down this same avenue and dined just across the street. It was horrible. Everything was horrible. The waiter was almost a no-show. He would drop in on us from time to time just to make sure we hadn't left. He would disappear, and after a long time of stretching our necks around looking for him, and being thoroughly disgusted, he would reappear, doing just enough to keep us from leaving. Frustrating, to say the least. Not only that, but the food was bad! I do remember that. Looking back, I'm surprised we didn't get up and leave.

The Overflow of More!

So back to the place with the interesting iron fish on the wall. We were welcomed by a very charming waitress. She had a beautiful smile and was very polite. I'm not sure when I started the tradition of asking a server their name but tonight was no different. They have a thankless job. Sure, we give them a tip for their service and I guess that's supposed to be our thank you. But I've made it a point of finding out names. It's a special way to recognize a person. Immediately I've seen people who were not into their job at the moment, but then a breakthrough smile would happen. They feel a little more valued than just serving.

There are two people it pays to be nice to: people who prepare or serve your food and people who handle your airline luggage. (Think on that.) I've had the opportunity, on more than one occasion, to reap the reward of being sharp with them and then finding out they repaid me in a special way for my lack of kindness.

So, I asked her, "What's your name?" Her response caught me off guard. "More," she softly replied. "What was that?" It sounded like you said MORE, I asked. "Yes, Myrrh, my father named me Myrrh, but, in Israel, we pronounce it More." I said, "Wait, your name is Myrrh, but it's pronounced More?" "I never knew that," I said. Myrrh is More and More Myrrh? I've always pronounced Myrrh like MEEEEERRRR, not MORE!

The rest of the evening, I just couldn't get that out of my mind. Myrrh and More. The More of Myrrh. The beauty of this young lady and her sweet way of serving was very charming. I asked her if she knew why her father named her such a unique name. She said, "It was a very special spice and perfume that was used in the temple. Part of the spices mixed for the holy anointing oil. And he has always told me how special I am and wanted me to know that God has an amazing future for me." What a wonderful answer, and what a great father, in imparting purpose into the life of his daughter.

Myrrh was the perfect hostess. She was kind, polite, and punctual. She didn't bother us, and she made sure the next course of the dinner was served with genuine care and was on time.

Ten Feet

That night, walking back to our hotel, we passed the horrible restaurant from the night before. The two establishments were at opposite ends of the dining spectrum. One was amazing, the other was not and only ten feet separated the two. Ten feet across a cobblestone street. On one side was a delicious culinary encounter facilitated by service from a wonderful hostess. On the other was a lackluster, terrible, who-cares disaster. The thought came to me of how many people are ten feet from the greatest moment of their life and they don't even know it? Ten feet from picking up your Bible. Ten feet from signing up to go on a mission trip. Ten feet from the altar of salvation. Ten feet from Jesus! Just ten feet from Eternal Life. It's like the contrast between Christ and Satan. How can anyone choose to follow such a bad and wicked master as the Devil? He's a thief and a liar. He's ripped you off again and again. He's never spoken a word of truth. Yet people file into his establishment and sit at his table and allow him to serve up the same old garbage, day after day after day.

"You are of your father the devil, and you want to do the desires of your father. He was a murderer from the beginning, and does not stand in the truth, because there is no truth in him. When he lies, he speaks from his own nature, for he is a liar and the father of lies." (John 8:44 MEV)

We All Have a Choice

Living in the overflow involves making a choice. The greatest choice of your life. Deciding to sit with Christ or sit with Satan. When I was a child Mom and Dad made all my decisions. They chose where I would sit. What I would do. Where I would go and what I would wear. They chose everything for me. They had even prayed for me before I was born and when I was born they dedicated me to God. Their hope was that when I would get older I would accept Christ as Savior. I made that choice at eleven years old, and I have been living for Christ for a lifetime.

You have a choice. Will you choose a life with Christ or a life with Satan? Truth or lies? You may be ten feet away from sitting at the table of the Lord. Hearing His voice. Receiving His precious life-giving fellowship. He's waiting for you.

"Behold, I stand at the door and knock. If anyone hears My voice and opens the door, I will come in to him and dine with him, and he with Me. ²¹ To him who overcomes I will grant to sit with Me on My throne, as I also overcame and sat down with My Father on His throne." (Revelation 3:20-21 NKJV)

If you've never received Christ as your Savior, you can right now. Ask Him to forgive you of your sin. Acknowledge you are a sinner in need of His love and life. Believe in your heart that

Christ died and rose from the dead for your salvation! Declare Him Lord over your life. Then start living in the overflow of His love.

Here's a Little Myrrh - MORE

At that meal on Ben-Yejuda Street, I remember thinking about the Holy Spirit. How He serves perfectly and how kindly He waits as we make good and bad decisions. How He warns us about things that might harm us. And I'm sure He celebrates, and I know He pours through us, as we yield our lives to the Lord.

"And they sat down to eat a meal. Then they lifted their eyes and looked, and there was a company of Ishmaelites, coming from Gilead with their camels, bearing spices, balm, and myrrh, on their way to carry *them* down to Egypt." (Genesis 37:25 NKJV)

In Genesis, Joseph is a type of Christ. He is sold by his brothers into slavery. We have sold our Lord for the cost of our sin. He was betrayed for silver. Christ was betrayed for silver. At the beginning of this journey he is carried off to Egypt with the scent of myrrh surrounding him. It was the gift of the Magi who brought gold, frankincense and myrrh. (Matthew 2:11) The young baby Christ would have been carried off with the same smells and possibly took the same route to Egypt when Herod was drawing down with his soldiers to murder the innocents of Bethlehem.

Worship Thirsts at the Cross

When Christ declares "I thirst, "at the cross, myrrh was mixed with wine. This mixture became like a narcotic to dull the senses and might cause the pain to be eased. This was offered to Christ on the cross. Yet He refused.

"Then they gave Him wine mingled with myrrh to drink, but He did not take it." (Mark 15:23 NKJV)

Christ did not choose to lessen the agony. He did not seek a shortcut for our salvation. The overflow of His love was worship to His Father. He offered Himself as the greatest living sacrifice. How much more should we offer ourselves to Him?

Paul the Apostle draws a powerful picture of that worship for the believer in Christ. We thirst for the cross. We thirst for a glimpse of Him in His moments of suffering. We desire the light of the cross to shine on us in our journey. We want to live in the overflow of the cross.

"I appeal to you therefore, brothers, by the mercies of God, to present your bodies as a living sacrifice, holy and acceptable to God, which is your spiritual worship. ² Do not be conformed to this world, but be transformed by the renewal of your mind, that by testing you may discern what is the will of God, what is good and acceptable and perfect." (Romans 12:1-2 ESV)

Worship Brings Forgiveness

When we stay at the cross of Christ we will hear Him say, "...Forgive them, for they do not know what they do."
(Luke 23:34a NKJV)

We are amazed! He forgives those who are causing this grief? He forgives the crucifiers?! He forgives the ones who hate him. He forgives those who plotted his death. He forgives the curses. He forgives me! He gives us hope. He gives life! He transforms the moment from death to life. I can't help but worship Him, because I am a part of those who are responsible. It is because of my sin that He was crucified. He forgave me at the cross. Thank you, Jesus, for that forgiveness!

Worship Brings Anointing

There is an anointing that overflows from worship. As we worship and spend time with the Lord an anointing of His power will rest on us. In the Book of Exodus, Moses gives instruction for the key ingredients of the anointing oil. It was a holy ointment that would be applied by the priest and on the holy objects.

"Also take for yourself quality spices—five hundred *shekels* of liquid myrrh, half as much sweet-smelling cinnamon (two hundred and fifty *shekels*), two hundred and fifty *shekels* of sweet-smelling cane, (Exodus 30:23 NKJV)

I believe there is an anointing that abides on the life of a believer in Christ. The oil Moses prepared was an externally applied oil for the priest, but this is an anointing that is applied internally by the Holy Spirit. It is reflective in the ministry and fruit of the believer. It flows out of a heart broken and ready for ministry.

Worship Brings Repentance

Genuine worship flows from a broken and ready heart. A thief declares, "remember me…" Remember me when you enter your Kingdom. We are unworthy. We are sinners needing a Savior! Worship brings repentance.

We see the crucifixion scene with brokenness. How is this possible? How could God send His Son to this? "For God so loved the world that He gave His only begotten Son, that who ever believes in Him should not perish but have everlasting life." (John 3:16 NKJV)

We see the instruments of brokenness. The hammer, the nails, the twisted crown of thorns, the blood-soaked clothing and the broken body of Christ. We can see the used spikes that have pierced through the flesh. They are splattered with blood and marked with the fingerprints of men bent on death.

Those hands were not raised in praise but were brutally affixing Him to the cross. Those are our hands. The long nails are motionless and holding His lifeless body. Sunlight hits the drops of blood. Bruised and beaten, the body of Christ sags under the weight of the finished agony. His face is marred and bruised. We can't recognize Him. He is no longer the man we saw hours before at the Last Supper.

Mary the mother of Jesus, Mary Magdalene and John are there. All are weeping and grieving. Grieving for the loss they feel. How will they overcome this grief? How can we overcome our grief? Is it through our overflow of repentance that we see His greater purpose in this moment? His purpose to bring us to a place of contrition? Not a grief for the cross but a grief that we failed to realize this love before.

Worship Lingers at the Cross

Do the words of resurrection seem foreign and forgotten to them? Do they attempt to move closer to Him? They want to touch Him, but they are frozen in fear. Do they dare advance toward Him? What will the soldiers do? The darkness has lifted. The effects of the earthquake have ended. Soldiers stand and stare. One kneels and prays. A weeping mother cries. The accusers are gone. Their vicious voices are silent now. What now? What will we do? Where will we go? Who will step in and do something? Say something? The questions at the cross are many? How could He love us?

We stare in amazement at such love. Worship lingers at the cross. We dare not disturb this holy moment. As we lift our voices in worship we are in awe of its beauty and its price. It has cost Heaven the ultimate price. We linger. We wait. Our hearts are breaking.

Worship Rises to the Cross

While others walk away, two men approach. They are speaking to the soldiers and showing a document. With a flip of the hand the centurion gives charge to release the corpse. It is lifeless. Destroyed by the spectacle of the slaughter. What value remains? Nothing of the man we knew is visible. The men bring with them a ladder and hurry to begin the work of removing the body. Gently, they free the hands and feet of the nails. These are not Galilean followers. These are well-dressed and notable temple leaders. What are they doing here with their fine tunics and robes? Where are they taking Him? Yet they work with such care. They gently ease the body from its pose. It seems etched forever in our minds. These men are now covered in the effects of the crucifixion. Their priestly robes are ruined. The blood has soaked through and stained their garments. But they act as if it's not an issue.

"After this, Joseph of Arimathea, being a disciple of Jesus, but secretly, for fear of the Jews, asked Pilate that he might take away the body of Jesus; and Pilate gave *him* permission. So, he came and took the body of Jesus. [39] And Nicodemus, who at first came to Jesus by night, also came, bringing a mixture of myrrh and aloes, about a hundred pounds. [40] Then they took the body of Jesus and bound it in strips of linen with the spices, as the custom of the Jews is to bury. [41] Now in the place where

He was crucified there was a garden, and in the garden a new tomb in which no one had yet been laid. [42] So there they laid Jesus, because of the Jews' Preparation *Day,* for the tomb was nearby." (John 19:38-42 NKJV)

The worship of Joseph and Nicodemus catch our attention. They rise to lift Him. We must rise to the cross. Our worship rises at the cross. The depth of love. The call of love. The amazing grace shed for us. Our worship rises in tones of love!

Worship Wants More of Jesus

Joseph and Nicodemus carefully prepare the body of Christ for burial, followed by John and Mary the mother of Christ and Mary Magdalene. The five of them remove themselves with the body. Nearby Joseph of Arimathea owns a garden, and in that place, stonecutters recently finished a tomb. It is getting late in the afternoon. We must hurry. But we can't rush this. We can't expedite worship. The burial cloths are brought. The 100 pounds of spices are generously applied to the wounds and bound in the shroud. We stare at the wounds.

With tears of worship and extravagance of effort the body is prepared. It is wiped and cleaned of the residue of the coagulated blood. Psalms and prayers are recited, and the atmosphere is filled with the aroma of myrrh and aloes.

Worship Gives Birth to Generosity

Generously the mixture is applied to the Lord's body. Historians tell us that the normal amount of weight of myrrh and aloes used at this time in Jewish tradition was about twenty pounds. That would be a luxurious preparation adornment. Many would be buried with very little or none at all, but this treasure of one hundred pounds of myrrh and aloes was great. This offering would have been immense. $150,000 to $200,000 would be the equivalent market value today of the myrrh and aloes that Nicodemus gave. For some in the modern day, that would be three to four times their annual income. It could be the cost of a home. For others it's the tuition for a child's education. For many it would be greater than their life savings. This is the offering Nicodemus brings, in this treasure of myrrh and aloes. This bag that will be poured out upon the body of his Master, then sealed in a tomb.

Nicodemus has come a long way from the night visit, where he asks Jesus, "Rabbi, we know that you are a teacher come from God, for no one can do these signs that you do unless God is with him." [3] Jesus answered him, "Truly, truly, I say to you, unless one is born again he cannot see the kingdom of God." (John 3:2b-3 ESV)

He is no longer a late-night visitor to Christ. He's not a channel-surfing seeker; he has stepped up to front-row leader. He is one of two that come for the body of Christ. How many thousands thronged Christ at His triumphal entry or sat on the mount and received the fish and loaves, and now only two come? Where are the faithful followers? Two come for the body of Christ?

Great love sacrifices greatly. Great love gives all. He has put his wealth, his name, his reputation and future into this moment. He identifies with Jesus. Jesus is Lord! He is no longer lurking in the shadows. He has come into the true light and now carries the wounded, broken, dead body of Christ his Savior. He has become a true worshiper.

Strangely enough, his worship is almost missed in the Gospel accounts. John is the only one to even mention the abundance of myrrh and aloes he brings. Could it be because John the

Apostle was one of the first to enter the tomb after the Resurrection, that he includes this in his writing? That when he and Peter entered the tomb, the aroma of Nicodemus' worship still lingered? Not the pungent smell of rotting flesh, but the one hundred pounds of sweet-smelling myrrh and aloes. Oh, that my *worship* would linger at the tomb. That the immense glory of His sacrifice would fill the tomb of my heart. That the resurrection of Christ in me would linger longer!

Worship Releases an Aroma

Joseph and Nicodemus hurriedly prepared the body of Christ for burial. Yet the aroma of the worship lingers. It fills the area inside and outside of the tomb. I pray that my worship for the Master would linger at the tomb. That the fragrance of what I've brought to Him will be evident. That I would be so filled with awe and wonder at His sacrifice that I would desire to follow His loving example. It's this overflow of worship that fills the empty tomb. Its worship that cannot be contained. That shouldn't be restricted to a place of death. It's the resurrected Christ that releases the aroma of worship. It's because He lives we live. With His resurrection comes worship!

Because He gave we can give. Because He was willing to die for us, we are willing to live for Him. It's the heart of worship that fills the empty.

"For a day in Your courts is better
than a thousand elsewhere.
I had rather be a doorkeeper in the house of
my God
than to dwell in
the tents of wickedness.
[11] For the Lord God is a sun and shield;
the Lord will give
favor and glory,
for no good thing will He withhold
from the one who walks uprightly.
[12] O Lord of Hosts,
blessed is the man
who trusts in You."
Psalm 84:10-12 MEV

Worship!

John 4:24 MEV
"God is Spirit, and those who worship Him must worship Him in spirit and truth."

Crossroads Fellowship

Study Guide Questions for Chapter 5

Worship in the Overflow
WORSHIP flows from the OVERFLOW of the HOLY SPIRIT!

Worshiping in the OVERFLOW doesn't just happen. If we truly desire the overflow of God's presence, we must allow the overflow of worship to flow out of our hearts.

Psalm 96:6a ESV
"Worship the Lord in the splendor of holiness;"

Describe a <u>Great Breakthrough</u> the Lord Gave You.

_____
_____
_____
_____
_____

John 8:44b MEV
"When he lies, he speaks from his own nature, for he is a liar and the father of lies."

How Has the Devil <u>Lied</u> to You?

_____
_____
_____
_____
_____

How Has Worship <u>Changed</u> You?

_____
_____
_____

Psalm 95:6 ESV
"Oh come, let us worship and bow down; let us kneel before the Lord, our Maker!"

Romans 12:1-2 ESV
"I appeal to you therefore, brothers, by the mercies of God, to present your bodies as a living sacrifice, holy and acceptable to God, which is your spiritual worship. ² Do not be conformed to this world, but be transformed by the renewal of your mind, that by testing you may discern what is the will of God, what is good and acceptable and perfect."

What Happens When <u>YOU</u> Worship?

_____
_____
_____
_____

What is One of Your <u>Favorite </u>Scriptures About Worship?

_____
_____
_____
_____

What Does the Overflow of Worship Mean to You?

_____
_____
_____
_____

John 4:23 ESV
"But the hour is coming, and is now here, when the true worshipers will worship the Father in spirit and truth, for the Father is seeking such people to worship him."

John 7:37:38 NKJV

"On the last day, that great day of the feast, Jesus stood and cried out, saying, "If anyone thirsts, let him come to Me and drink. ³⁸ He who believes in Me, as the Scripture has said, out of his heart will flow rivers of living water."

Chapter 6

Overload

We will NEVER experience the OVERFLOW if we Live in the OVERLOAD.

"And He said unto them, come ye yourselves apart into a desert place, and rest a while: for there were many coming and going, and they had no leisure so much as to eat." (Mark 6:31 KJV)

O verload happens to everyone. Every leader, pastor, parent, teacher, administrator, student, and person alive will feel overload at some point. Overload is draining, but overflow is refreshing.

In Mark 6 Jesus and the disciples find themselves at a new place. They have come to the place He feels comfortable in sending them out, without His supervision. They are going out two by two into villages and teaching and ministering to the needs of the people. Their assignment is to take nothing with them and be ready for anything.

Verses twelve and thirteen of Chapter Six tell us, "And they went out, and preached that men should repent. [13] And they cast out many devils, and anointed with oil many that were sick, and healed them." (Mark 6:12-13 KJV)

This is exciting and wonderful. It's what they've waited for and hoped would happen. It's the genesis of new ministry and ministers. For all who have spent time in ministry going out preaching, praying and delivering it can be very rewarding.

With the spiritual high of ministering to people but also comes the toll it takes on your emotions. Not only that, many times I've felt physically exhausted. If you're not careful you will find yourself ministering from emptiness.

1979

August 1, 1979, was the date I began serving in full-time ministry. I was nineteen and green as a new cucumber. I was the new youth/children's/bus/bulletin/song leader/hospital/drama/school helper/outreach pastor. I've thought many times about how challenging and wonderful those early days were. It was a dream come true and I would do it all over again. If someone said, "We've invented a time machine and you can go back to any point and start over, I would do it today!" It was the hardest and most rewarding time of my life. I'd love to live this life all over again... not out of regret but out of wanting to watch God do this big thing He's done in me, all over again!

The 213th day of 1979 was a Wednesday. Why did I start on a Wednesday? I can't remember, but it will always be a marked date on my heart! What a glorious day! What a wonderful day!

Here's the other side of it all. I dove headlong into ministry. I volunteered to lead everything. I saw needs everywhere. It was my desire to meet every one of them. Nothing seemed impossible. However, months later, exhaustion started to set in. I found myself so busy my prayer life began to lack. Study in God's word was no longer the center of my morning. Busy? I was busy! I could do this! I can do that! I will do this! *I was in the ministry!* The problem was that OVERLOAD was setting in. I was getting more and more overloaded, until one day I could not do it. I had to stop.

When my overload spillway overflowed, it wasn't pretty. I was no longer excited. Truth be told, I was feeling a little bitter. I was not rejoicing; I was resisting. I was overwhelmed. I had bit off more than I could chew. I had no clue how to give some of it back. What I found out was you can keep signing up to lead the next big thing, and someone will always let you. I was trying to be the answer to everything. Impossible!

Ministry has to start with overflow, but it must remain in the overflow of the Holy Spirit. The disciples of Christ are experiencing the same. Overflow comes from the Lord! They were sent out from His presence. With His authority on them. Overload comes with trouble. Overload comes with heaviness. Overload can weigh you down.

Overflow Comes from Above!

For me as a pastor the most taxing time of the week is <u>after</u> I've preached three times Sunday morning and I've just left the guest experience and now I'm walking out into the commons. My mind is full of stuff. I'm physically shot. If I feel the services have gone well, I may feel exhilarated, but if something has not gone well, I may feel low. This can be an emotional roller coaster, and every person who ministers can feel this, or has felt this.

Here at Crossroads, we have so many who minister on our teams. Every one of them may feel a little overloaded and overwhelmed at times. Perhaps you've stood at the door greeting, or ushered in the sanctuary. Better yet you've stood in the hot parking lot for hours and welcomed the crowd. You might be filling in for a few people who didn't make it. You have been in serve mode for more than half the day. You're drained, exhausted, and might I say, probably a little HANGRY (hungry and angry and ready to eat). It's 1:45 p.m. and that last car is leaving the parking lot. You are ready to head to the house. Out of nowhere, someone needs you. It's another worker. They haven't had time for any prayer or ministry to them and you're it. It's a real exceptional need. It's paramount that you stop and minister. This person needs help - NOW!

You implore of the Lord, "Don't let this overload me, help me help this person" and at that moment the overflow kicks in. Somewhere down inside, the Holy Spirit helps you and you stay a little longer and you give a little more than what you thought you had. These are some of the best moments. I'm so proud of our teams and their love in helping the hurting. But it takes a team of PRAYING people serving in those areas to recognize the needs. Everyone is a minister at the Crossroads! Every Christian should be a minister wherever they are.

Overflow or Overload?

On the other side of overflow is overload. There are times when you've had a customer, you've had someone come into your office and when they leave, you are completely drained. I believe there are some people who have a greater *drain factor* than others. You know what I mean! It's that feeling you get when THAT person leaves. You are bone dry of all emotional energy! You feel the exhaustion in every question, or statement, and nothing is life-giving.

Ask yourself, "What drains me?" Because, what drains you may be tartar sauce to someone else. I love my daily prayer times. There's nothing more powerful than a few hours in the presence of the Lord. I love getting ready for the next sermon. It fills me up. I'm stoked about this coming week. I also love hunting and I love old cars. However, I have friends who hate hunting and know nothing about cars. They are into golf and fishing and something else I might struggle with.

My drain factor begins where endless draining questions start. Problems without solutions. Some people are good about delivering you a problem but have no clue how to come up with a solution.

They mindlessly ask you questions, and *they think*, because you are the <u>head</u> of the organization, you should have all the answers. I try to surround myself with solution people. Bring me a question but bring me a few suggested solutions with the problem. People who are high-capacity leaders think like this. These people are gold on any team! If they bring me a question or a problem they've already thought through several solutions. They are just not sure which solution is the best, and they want me to help with that final decision.

When it comes to being drained by something, it's best to hire people who have a gifting for an area you might lack. If you are a people person, then you might need some fact-checkers. People who can walk through the difficult land mines of all the details you just can't stand.

If you are an employee and you have a challenging day with your boss, ask yourself, "Am I being a drain on my employer's leadership style?" Perhaps I should look for what I can be to help him/her go to that next level, by helping in an area they might be weak in. It may be time to work on some new skills.

"Think for Me!"

That first pastor I worked with was my sweet father-in-law, Pastor Dan Heil. His favorite saying he used on me was, "Think for me!" When working on a construction project one day at the church, I was watching him and frustrating him, all at the same time. He would have to ask for everything. Hammer? Saw? Board? NAILS!?

Finally, he spoke pretty LOUDLY and yelled out, "Hey, think for me!" He stopped and looked at me and said, "Can't you see what I'm about to do?" I was shocked he spoke so loudly at me. All of sudden I started really trying to watch what he was trying to do, and I said, with a little hesitation, "You're about to cut that board?" He said, "YES! So, what should I have waiting on me?" I said, "A saw?" "YES! Think for me! Watch what I'm doing and think for me." That was some pretty great advice. From then on, I tried to think for whoever I served in ministry with. What do they need next? How can I help them fulfill what they are trying to do?

It started to set me apart. I would even drop by the pastor's office and ask, "You need anything pastor?" One senior pastor told me a few years ago, "Out of all the people who worked for me, you were the only one who would ask me if there was there anything I needed." I give thanks to Pastor Heil and his mentoring me to have a great work ethic and teaching me about being an armor bearer.

As I started trying to think for him, I could see things he needed far in advance of the need. I would get there earlier. I would try to help him with the little things. I later learned the load a lead pastor has. It is heavy. Leadership is very heavy. A lot is on your mind and your heart. You have a lot of people counting on you. You can't allow the overload to cripple what you are trying to do. If you are a helper, administration, department leader, secretary or volunteer you can try to think for that leader. Who knows? You may be the answer they've prayed for.

Overhaulin'

Being a car guy I love the classic hot rods. I'm not really into the new mega sports cars, but the oldies I love. I have a girlfriend and she's a 1965 red mustang coupe. She's called Whoa Nellie!

When we bought her nine years ago, I jokingly told my wife Danielle that she would never have to worry about where my girlfriend lives. I said and laughed. "She lives in the garage." She's been a work in progress for years.

So I loved to watch the show "Overhaulin.' It lasted for ten seasons. I think they are bringing it back. I still love the reruns, but the host of the show was Chip Foose. The show's premise was that an unknowing "victim" – the mark, in the show's language – is nominated to be overhauled" by his or her family or friends, the insiders. The mark's car, usually an old and tired antique car, was obtained through some ruse. Throughout the show they show you the progress on the overhaul. They'll go from top to bottom on the vehicle and it will be virtually new by the end of the show. Then they will surprise the mark with his overhauled classic.

In car terms... we need some *OVERHAULIN'!*

To get back into the overflow you may need to overhaul your schedule. You might need to set aside some good, quiet, quality time with just you and the Lord. If your marriage is suffering the same goes for you and your spouse. For whatever area of your life that may seem overwhelmed or overloaded you should think about putting your life up on the lift and checking out what's underneath. You could be due a good overhaul!

"And He said unto them, come ye yourselves apart into a desert place, and rest a while." (Mark 6:31a KJV)

I've heard it said, *"if you don't come apart and rest you'll eventually come apart."*

We all need to renew ourselves or the draining will continue until we are overloaded. The Scripture goes on to say, "for there were many coming and going, and they had no leisure so much as to eat." (Mark 6:31b KJV) You get the sense that the only place they can get a clear time of rest is just the far-off deserted places. They couldn't even find a place to stop and eat because so many were coming around.

An Oasis in a Desert Place

Something needs to be said about just finding a resting place. It's the place you stop from the daily grind. It's not a bad place. It's your place to escape for a bit. It's not an immoral place. It's your recharge station. Besides having an old car to tinker with, a few years ago, Danielle and I bought a little piece of property about 6 – 7 hours away from Houston. It's an oasis to me. It's remote. I get there, and I recharge. There are a lot of deer and other wildlife in the area. To some it's just a place in the wilderness. They might think, it's a desert. I even love the drive. It renews me.

When I was NEW to the ministry, we didn't make the money we do now, so buying a hot rod or some land would have been out of the question. But an oasis place might be going to lunch with a friend. It might be a movie or date with your spouse. It's away from the grind of it all. What's remote from your job? Your oasis might be golfing, fishing, painting, cooking or watching a movie. The overload will destroy you if you don't retreat sometime.

Listen, I love a big crowd at the church just like the rest of you pastors. But I don't resent it when my church family gets away for a holiday. I try and always say, "Good for you!" I truly mean it. We all need to get away sometime. However, some have too many holidays, if you know what I mean? If you don't get away, the overload will destroy you. Your church family needs renewal also. Don't resent them. Allow them to get refreshed so they can come back charged also. I ask my staff to take time off. I love to see them take time off each week. It's not always possible, but it's the idea of what we're shooting for.

When I get overloaded I become my worst enemy. And if you're not careful, a lot of staff start off this way. They want to help so much that they sign up for too much at the beginning. Then, when frustration and burnout are finished you have a staff member who hates his/her assignment and the only recourse is to go somewhere else.

The overflow of ministry has to be refreshed. I was drained. <u>I was working *at* the ministry, not *in* the ministry.</u> Burnout was all over me. If we didn't have a meeting all those years ago to address my workload, I would not be here today. We did have a very productive meeting, the discussion happened, and I got some relief.

Truthfully, sometimes we put too much on ourselves. No one else demanded you be here that early or that late. No one else knows you've been here that many days in a row unless it becomes a conversation. Overload is very real.

Strained

[*Jesus Predicts Peter's Denial*] "And the Lord said, "Simon, Simon! Indeed, Satan has asked for you, that he may sift *you* as wheat. **32** But I have prayed for you, that your faith should not fail; and when you have returned to *Me,* strengthen your brethren." **33** But he said to Him, "Lord, I am ready to go with You, both to prison and to death." **34** Then He said, "I tell you, Peter, the rooster shall not crow this day before you will deny three times that you know Me." (Luke 22:31-34 NKJV)

Years ago, I was on a mission trip in Peru. We were in a little village and we came across a lady sitting on the ground, with a pile of grain in front of her. The grain was on a grass woven rug, the size of a doormat. She was sitting with her legs crossed in front of her, and she was beating the grain. Then she would throw it in the air. The wind was blowing a little and the broken pieces of husk would fly away. The missionary I was with said, "Do you know what she's doing?" I said, "No." "Sifting wheat!" He said. Remember the story of Jesus with Peter? As I watched her, I thought about how many times have I've felt like I was being sifted. Beaten, thrown in the air and falling back to the ground! Everything is up and then crashing down. You probably understand too well.

A modern word for sift might be to be "STRAINED." When we cook, we sometimes use a colander to strain the juice or water off vegetables and noodles. You turn on the fire and bring the water to a boil then it's poured out and strained and then the cold water runs over it... That feels like life when you're overloaded and overwhelmed. You're in the fire and being boiled alive, then you're strained through little tiny metal holes, and then a huge letdown hits you. The straining or sifting is you being filtered or separated. When we experience the filtering of a trial we <u>can</u> come out on top. We have to see that the things we lost we really needed to lose anyway. We needed arrogance and pride sifted and strained off.

Straining can also mean excessive effort. If we will live in the overflow we've got to *stop trying to **make** things happen*. We are straining. We feel like if I try harder it will work better. If I do this or that I can make it more impressive. If I have different lights or a different set on stage, it'll go over bigger and better.

No Sweat

"And it shall be, whenever they enter the gates of the inner court, that they shall put on linen garments; no wool shall come upon them while they minister within the gates of the inner court or within the house." (Ezekiel 44:17 NKJV)

In Ezekiel 44, we see a picture of the garments of the priesthood. The priesthood shall wear linen, not wool. One is light and airy and the other is hot and heavy. The linen garments cause you to stay cool. The wool garments are for warmth, but you can get too hot and start sweating. What a picture of what ministry in the overflow should look like! Ministry should be without sweat and straining to make it work. It should be without my excessive effort. It's not Mike's ministry anyway. It's the Lord's ministry.

[A Song of Ascents of Solomon.] "Unless the Lord builds the house, they labor in vain who build it; Unless the Lord guards the city, the watchman stays awake in vain."
(Psalm 127:1 NKJV)

Ministry in the Overflow Should Lift Us

<u>Note it's called a song of ascent.</u>   This is how we are to approach the Lord's house. "Unless the Lord builds the house…" He builds the house. It's not mine, it's His. "…they labor in vain who build it." I've got to stop straining and making it from my effort. Let Him just use me. "Unless the Lord guards the city, the watchman stays awake in vain." The Lord is the one watching over this. He's the guard! Not me. I can stay awake and worry and be exhausted over all I've got to do or have to pay for. The Lord's not worried so why should I?

In 2017, a dear friend and saint of our church graduated to Heaven. Her name was Lucy Gates. She was a treasure. She loved me, and she loved Crossroads. I called her our CEO. Chief Encouraging Officer! She was amazing! Before her memorial I asked her family if I could look through her Bible. It was wonderful!   All the pages had amazing little sayings and clippings. I recopied one of those sayings, into the front of my Bible.

You can never conquer pride until you can do nothing - be nobody – and be content. Know who you are in Christ.

What controls you doesn't control Him.
What troubles you doesn't trouble Him.
What fatigues you doesn't fatigue Him.

Ministry in the Overflow Should Encourage!

This is a good word for pastors. Hear what I'm saying. The ministry should be your greatest joy. Stop sweating over stuff you have no control over. Let the linen of the Holy Spirit clothe you. Don't sweat! Don't worry! Don't fret! It's the Lord's work.

Recently, as a church, we had given and given to missions. It's just who we are. We were sending teams on mission trips and all our funds were tapped out. We needed a great offering that week and it was the middle of summer. I prayed and asked the Lord, "We've been giving and giving Lord. Crossroads needs your help!" That weekend someone dropped in a $30,000 tithe, *above the regular giving. It was just enough to remind me. I see you, and I know* where you are, and it's going to be all right. Don't worry.

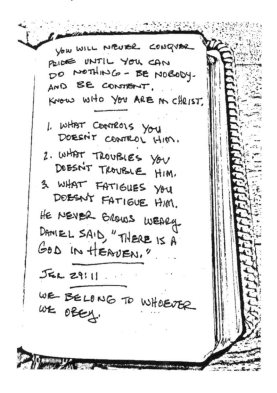

Study Guide Questions for Chapter 6

Overload

We will NEVER experience the OVERFLOW,
if we Live in the OVERLOAD.

Overload happens to everyone. Every leader, pastor, parent, teacher, administrator, student, and person alive will feel overload at some point. Overload is draining, but overflow is refreshing.

Mark 6:31 KJV
"And He said unto them, come ye yourselves apart into a desert place, and rest a while: for there were many coming and going, and they had no leisure so much as to eat."

What Causes Overload in Your Life?

_____
_____
_____
_____
_____

Do I Cause Others to Experience Overload?

_____
_____
_____
_____
_____

Psalm 127:1 NKJV
[A Song of Ascents of Solomon.] "Unless the Lord builds the house, they labor in vain who build it; Unless the Lord guards the city, the watchman stays awake in vain."

What Creates Fresh Overflow?

_____
_____
_____
_____
_____

How Can I <u>Create Fresh Overflow</u> for Others?

_____
_____
_____
_____
_____

Nehemiah 8:10 ESV
"Then he said to them, "Go your way. Eat the fat and drink sweet wine and send portions to anyone who has nothing ready, for this day is holy to our Lord. And do not be grieved, for the joy of the Lord is your strength."

Write Out a Prayer Request of What You Need Encouragement in. Sometimes We Just Need the Lord to Remind Us He Hasn't Forgotten Us.

_____
_____
_____
_____
_____

Philippians 4:19 NKJV
"And my God shall supply all your need according to His riches in glory by Christ Jesus."

Overflow is About Giving!

*Each Year We Give Our Church Family
Many Opportunities to Support Local and Global Missions.*

Children from our school in Kenya wanting to be close.

Chapter 7

Overflow Determines Direction

Great FOCUS happens in the OVERFLOW
of the Holy Spirit.

When we lose sight, we can stumble and fall. A greater focus in life comes from seasons of extended fellowship with the Holy Spirit. That fellowship will increase a godly direction.

"Then Jesus was led up into the wilderness by the Spirit to be tempted by the devil" (Matthew 4:1 MEV)

What a strange verse. Jesus being led by the Spirit into the wilderness, to be tempted by the devil. I believe that everything God does is good and perfect, but this was a little troubling the first time I read it. Even now, one could ask why? Why a wilderness? Why tempted by the devil? For what purpose?

Could the "why" be, why shouldn't we expect to face the enemy? Everything God has ever created has been attacked by the enemy: the home, marriage, family, birth, life, healing and the future have all been in the crosshairs of the devil. Herod's soldiers were dispatched to Bethlehem when Jesus was just an infant. The baby Moses was hidden because the enemy tried to snuff out that leader's life before he ever became a boy. Every new ministry will face the wilderness and it will face the enemy trying to destroy it before it ever gets started. *The enemy will always try to abort what God is giving birth to.* Jesus will walk through the wilderness and a holy resolve will come upon Him. He will emerge determined to move forward in the direction His Father has sent Him.

Tempted

If Christ was tempted, we too will face temptation. If Christ was in the wilderness we will walk through the same. If He was hungry, we will hunger and thirst for more of the Father. In all points He would pass the tests. And we follow His steps. If He emerges with greater resolution to follow His Father, we need the same dedication to commit to His commission.

"Blessed *is* the man who endures temptation; for when he has been approved, he will receive the crown of life which the Lord has promised to those who love Him. [13] Let no one say when he is tempted, "I am tempted by God"; for God cannot be tempted by evil, nor does He Himself tempt anyone. [14] But each one is tempted when he is drawn away by his own desires and enticed. [15] Then, when desire has conceived, it gives birth to sin; and sin, when it is full-grown, brings forth death. [16] Do not be deceived, my beloved brethren. [17] Every good gift and every perfect gift is from above, and comes down from the Father of lights, with whom there is no variation or shadow of turning. [18] Of His own will He brought us forth by the word of truth, that we might be a kind of firstfruits of His creatures." (James 1:12-18 NKJV)

Tried

There is temptation and then there is testing. We are tested for the use of future ministry, but temptation is from the enemy. The testing defines the character of the leader. The temptation is used by the enemy to accuse the leader of his weakness. It's to laugh at his failure, but the test is to identify the weakness without condemnation. The test helps bring the weakness to the surface so that it can be dealt with. Perhaps it's a weakness that needs to be confessed and forgiven.

The enemy chooses times of temptation when we are weak.
God uses testing moments to bring forth strength.
The flesh is deceitful and promotes ego, pride and self.
The Spirit is truth and reveals ego, pride and selfish ambition.
The flesh fights against the presence of God.
The Holy Spirit releases power to overcome the flesh.

Depending on what you yield yourself to, that will determine who will win, the flesh or the Spirit, and that will determine the direction of your life.

Testing is needed. Testing is valuable. What use is a great sword until it has been folded over and over in the furnace of the blacksmith? It must be hardened. It must be tempered and tried. When it is properly prepared the finished sword will cut with precision. Skip a step and it will crack, split or even break apart. How dangerous for us to miss one of the steps the Lord has for us.

The purpose of the test is greater than the moment. The moment seems hard and unfair, but it is for the good of the warrior, to be ready for the greater battle. Some battles are staging grounds for the greater.

Spirit-Led

But just as there are days when the temptations and trials seem to pile up, there are many wonderful Spirit-led days. Days He is guiding and it's apparent that this is not a wilderness. This is the fellowship of the Holy Spirit.

One of the greatest joys of being a believer in Christ is being led by the Spirit. You are at the right place at the right time, and many times you had no idea it was even happening.

"The steps of a good man are ordered by the Lord, And He delights in His way."   (Psalm 37:23 NKJV)

I've walked into a hospital room at the exact moment I needed to be there. I've called and someone said to me, "How did you know?" I've arrived at the exact moment a dear saint was making their graduation to glory. To be a comfort to a hurting family. The prompting of the Spirit is a gift to be enjoyed and deployed by believers in Christ.

Many times, I am totally unaware the Holy Spirit has set me up to encounter a need. What a privilege for the Spirit to give direction and to lead us. If I knew all He had planned for a day I would fret and worry, but living and walking in the Spirit is living in the overflow. Living in the overflow is about following the leadership of the Holy Spirit. It's also learning to hear His voice and know His plan.

"*There is* therefore now no condemnation to those who are in Christ Jesus, who do not walk according to the flesh, but according to the Spirit."   (Romans 8:1 NKJV)

As believers in Christ we are not living in condemnation any more. We are free from that. We are no longer walking in the fleshly mind but in the mind of Christ. We walk according to the Spirit as our Lord Jesus Christ did, 2,000 years ago.

Baptism

"Then Jesus came from Galilee to John at the Jordan to be baptized by him. [14] But John prohibited Him, saying, "I need to be baptized by You, and do You come to me?" [15] But Jesus answered him, "Let it be so now, for it is fitting for us to fulfill all righteousness." Then he permitted Him. [16] And when Jesus was baptized, He came up immediately out of the water. And suddenly the heavens were opened to Him, and He saw the Spirit of God descending on Him like a dove. [17] And a voice came from heaven, saying, "This is My beloved Son, in whom I am well pleased." (Matthew 3:13-17 MEV)

Standing on the bank of the Jordan River that day must have been quite the scene. People stretching to see the prophet preaching. The splashing. The declarations of repentance. Tears of joy from those coming up from the water. Perhaps hundreds or even thousands were there. The Scriptures do not give evidence of that detail, but we know this is the place of John's ministry.

Then it is as if a pause in the action takes place. A man walks toward the water. A man who is free from sin. John knows this man! Receiving Him into the water, John declares his own unworthy status. A very short discussion happens, then John obediently baptizes the Son of God. At that moment, the most extraordinary thing happens. At that moment, on cue, the heavens opened, and the most brilliant light shines on the two. Descending and unfolding in front of everyone comes the appearance of a heavenly dove, toward Jesus. Then a voice said, "This is My beloved Son, in whom I am well pleased." Hands begin to lift in the crowd toward heaven. John shouts praise to Jehovah's mighty name. Some whisper the name of God. Others begin to recite prayers of praise. It is a wonderful scene.

A Heavenly Suddenly

"SUDDENLY" the heavens opened to Him. The Spirit brought Jesus to this place where John was baptizing. When we follow the leading of the Holy Spirit we will have a "suddenly" moment. The heavens open to those who follow His direction. Wouldn't it be great to see the physical manifestation of the blessing?

Many times, I've watched the overflow of heaven come down on the face of a person I am praying for. Heavenly Father, give us a heavenly suddenly! Show up suddenly and pour your presence on your people. Suddenly be in our midst. Suddenly bring peace. Suddenly bring healing. Suddenly bring rest. I love the heavenly suddenly!

This is definitely a high place to celebrate in Jesus' life. At our spiritual high places, we need the same affirming moments with the Father. He speaks to us. The heavenly suddenly refreshes us. We hear His voice. We feel His touch on our hearts. We long for the heavenly suddenly moments. This is a great day. It's such a celebration. We celebrate the Son of God has come.

Rockstar Savior?

You might think Jesus would linger and wait around with the crowd and allow people to touch Him. This is His water baptism. His coming-out party. This is the best time for His press secretary to issue a statement. Where will He go from here? Where is the website announcement? Perhaps He will sign a few autographs. Set up a table with dove shirts and the screen print "My Beloved Son." Only $29.95 with HIS signature. Surely, He realizes how big a deal this is? Security! He needs security surrounding Him! Someone may get too close, and someone may stay too long. I'm sure His private jet is waiting to usher Him back to Nazareth. This is amazing! We wait for the announcement. This is why God sent Him to be recognized as the Son of God! Right?

We will find no Rockstar Savior in Christ.
We will only find a humble servant.
The Lamb of God.

Overflow Determines Direction

Jesus was overflowing with the presence of the Father before He arrives at the Jordan. He has been led by the Spirit, up until this very moment. Here He will receive fresh the refilling overflow of His Father's love. All three members of the Godhead will be present at this meeting. The Father, Son and Holy Spirit will come together and celebrate the beginning of this new day. But as quickly as the moment happens it is over. He leaves without fanfare. Without anyone running up to Him. Only amazement at His humility and gentleness. He leaves the Jordan overflowing with the Holy Spirit and drawn to the wilderness. He must empty Himself of the flesh man and fill up the Spirit man. If the Master needs to empty Himself of the flesh man, then why don't we? Why don't we spend more time emptying ourselves of this world?

The Wilderness

"Then Jesus was led up into the wilderness by the Spirit to be tempted by the devil. [2] And He had fasted for forty days and forty nights, and then He was hungry. [3] And the tempter came to Him and said, "If You are the Son of God, command that these stones be turned into bread." [4] But He answered, "It is written, 'Man shall not live by bread alone, but by every word that proceeds out of the mouth of God.'" [5] Then the devil took Him up into the holy city and set Him on the highest point of the temple, [6] and said to Him, "If You are the Son of God, throw Yourself down. For it is written, 'He shall give His angels charge concerning you,' and 'In their hands they shall lift you up, lest at any time you dash your foot against a stone.' [7] Jesus said to him, "It is also written, 'You shall not tempt the Lord your God.'" [8] Again, the devil took Him up on a very high mountain and showed Him all the kingdoms of the world and their grandeur, [9] and said to Him, "All these things I will give You if

You will fall down and worship me." [10] Then Jesus said to him, "Get away from here, Satan! For it is written, 'You shall worship the Lord your God, and Him only shall you serve.'" (Matthew 4:1-10 MEV)

The Spirit led Him into the wilderness. The wilderness is not a place of celebration like the baptismal pool. It's hot and dusty. No one stands with you in the wilderness. The wilderness is a lonely place. But God uses the wilderness to get our attention. The wilderness helps us focus on the important. We see the simple moving of the presence of God.

The wilderness is a place of trial. Why do we have to go there? The wilderness is the place of proving. It's the place of drawing out the dross from our hearts. Odd but the wilderness is a place of personal growth. The place of refinement. It's there in the wilderness that God speaks best. We can hear Him more clearly in the wilderness.

There are no surrounding noises. It's in the quiet wilderness of *nothing* that we must be led. Away from the bright lights, cell phones, social media, advertisements, and entertainment. Noise that deafens us to the gentle whisper of the Holy Spirit. The wilderness is a good place.

It's there that we find ourselves alone with God. Good things can happen in the wilderness. <u>God things can happen in the wilderness</u>. Without the prison cell of Philippi, Paul would not have been free to write Ephesians, Thessalonians and Colossians. It is joy in the midst of trouble. Because of the prison cell he was confined to that time to get some fresh writing completed. When do you have time to do that? It's in the depths of that cell in Philippi he pens these words:

"Nevertheless, you have done well that you shared in my distress. [15] Now you Philippians know also that in the beginning of the gospel, when I departed from Macedonia, no church shared with me concerning giving and receiving but you only. [16] For even in Thessalonica you sent *aid* once and again for my necessities. [17] Not that I seek the gift, but I seek the fruit that abounds to your account. [18] Indeed I [g]have all and abound. I am full, having received from Epaphroditus the things *sent* from you, a sweet-smelling aroma, an acceptable sacrifice, well pleasing to God. [19] And my God shall supply all your need according to His riches in glory by Christ Jesus." (Philippians 4:14-19 NKJV)

Part of the overflow of Paul's prison time in Philippi was the journey of generosity it takes the Macedonian believers on. They would be able to be a part and share in the ministry of Paul through giving to His needs. The heavenly fruit that would be credited to their account would abound!

And because they were faithful to give and serve he declares in verse 19:

"And my God shall supply all your need according to His riches in glory by Christ Jesus."

The Enemy of the Overflow

We must stay alert in the wilderness. Other voices will try to get our attention. The enemy loves the wilderness too. It's where He tries to tell us how unworthy we are. He throws our past at us. He exposes fears and weaknesses. He is the enemy of the overflow of God's presence. This enemy is a liar and has been from the beginning. Very aware of our weaknesses, he will try his best to get us to give in. He will argue with us in the wilderness. But the weaker our bodies become, the stronger our spirits can grow.

Many have fallen in the wilderness. Many have been unable to withstand the heat. Temptation wins. Instead of waiting for the overflow of the Lord's presence they allow overload and lust to fill them. Sometimes pride destroys them. At other times, it's arrogance. The enemy of the overflow will try everything to defeat a heart waiting for God. They may even try a shortcut out of their valley experience. Instead of staying for the full test they leave too soon and never really grasp the power the wilderness has of making the man.

The message that "God only wants to bless" is the enemy of the wilderness. I love to think on all the blessings of the Lord, but even through the wilderness we can come out blessed. But blessing is not a substitute for what we must face. We must walk through this season. Springtime is only one season. There is summer, fall and winter. These seasons have their purpose. God uses the wilderness. Don't fret and complain in the wilderness. God uses the wilderness to work on the budding time for the next growth period. It's important. It's not punishment - it's refinement. In the winter, dead branches break off and the tree can have new growth. It's healthy to shed some dead branches.

Wait for It!

Many times, I've watched a video just because it said at the top, "WAIT FOR IT!" Maybe it's a car wreck compilation of motorcycles gone wrong. I'm captivated by the title. I'm captivated by Moses' first wilderness journey. Like a wreck about to happen or a sweet reunion with a soldier's family, I don't' want to look away. I must watch.

In the Wilderness...

God Give Us Greater Focus!

A Focus of Deeper Worship
A Focus in a Greater Season of Prayer
A Focus to Read the Word
A Focus to Honor the Lord
A Focus to See the Will of God
A Focus to Hear What God is Saying
A Focus to Understand What's Next
A Focus to Find His Direction

On the other hand, the enemy always questions. He questions my motives. He questions my heart. He questions God. He asks, "Why would God do this if He loves you?" He questions my passion. He questions my desire. He questions the genuineness of my faith. When your mind fills with questions, remember who questions.

Jesus doesn't argue with the enemy. He quotes the Word. The Word of the Lord is Yes and Amen! The enemy's word is why? How? When? Being willing to wait and hear the voice of the Lord and see Him work could take some time. But if He speaks directly and quickly then get up and follow His instruction.

"Then the devil left Him, and immediately angels came and ministered to Him." (Matthew 4:11 MEV)

Following that season in the wilderness is a time of refreshment. Allow the angels of the Lord to minister to you. Allow the presence of the Lord to overflow. Perhaps there is a deeper relationship than before. A deeper trench of His presence now flows through you. You've found another well of salvation in the wilderness. You've experienced a greater level of love and understanding. The simple truth is bread and manna to your soul. Let the Lord speak to you in the wilderness.

I've had God confirm so much in the wilderness. Nothing is more clear than the sky in the wilderness. Some of the most beautiful scenery can be found in the desert.

"Do not remember the former things, Nor consider the things of old. [19] Behold, I will do a new thing, Now it shall spring forth; Shall you not know it? I will even make a road in the wilderness *And* rivers in the desert." (Isaiah 43:18-19 NKJV)

God can MAKE a ROAD in your wilderness!
He can MAKE a RIVER in your desert!
He's not limited.
He's not afraid.
He's not troubled.
He will declare "YES!"

When I spend quality days and weeks in the wilderness I receive divine instruction. Nothing can knock me down. My focus becomes crisp and clear. Question me, but I will not move from the resolve the Holy Spirit gives. It comes from the overflow. Even the questions I may still not have an answer for I don't worry over. I'm at peace with decisions and direction. There is a holy moment waiting in the wilderness for you.

Defining Moments

Thirty-Five Hundred years ago, a prophet was in the wilderness. He was in the incubator of the Holy Spirit. He's covered in the dust of forty years. Gone so long now from his former life, they've probably forgotten his name. He doesn't care anymore. He has a wife and a couple of children. It makes no difference to him. Life has moved on. The wilderness helps you remember, and it helps you forget.

The wilderness of failure is a killer. Who cares about you? Why should they? You doubt the call. I've seen many die in this wilderness. No one is a bigger failure than this man. Murderer. Fugitive. Failed prince of Egypt. Hebrew? We doubt the past words from the Lord!

Walking that wilderness, Moses must have felt God is finished with him. God doesn't know his name anymore. But the wilderness can't define Moses. The failure of Egypt can't define Moses. The murder haunts him. God must be finished with Him.

God's Not Finished with You

"For the gifts and the calling of God are irrevocable." (Romans 11:29 NKJV)

Moses stands and looks across the desert and an interesting sight catches his eye. Is it a flame? Is it a fire? He stares for a minute. Smoke? Flames? Is this just a flash fire and a move-on event? Or perhaps, it a lasting blaze that will take out what little vegetation is available? Should he move the flock? What should he do? He's watched fires spring up before, but as he watches, this fire is different. The source is centralized. There is a bush, but it is not consumed.

Holy Fire

God uses holy fire to get our attention. Let it be a beacon in our desert. Let it catch our attention. Let it burst upon the darkness of our depression and give direction to our future.

"Then Moses said, "I will now turn aside and see this great sight, why the bush does not burn." [4] So when the Lord saw that he turned aside to look, God called to him from the midst of the bush and said, "Moses, Moses!" And he said, "Here I am."   (Exodus 3:3-4 NKJV)

He focuses on the flame. He focuses on the bush. He focuses on the surroundings. It draws him from the rock he's resting against, high above the desert floor. He forgets his herd for a while. He moves toward the fire. What a strange sight.

It never ceases to amaze me the things God will use in our wilderness to get our attention. The overflow can come to us and change our direction in a moment.   The wilderness can have a great impact on our lives. This will be a defining moment. What God has been getting ready is complete. Israel needs a leader. God is sending this fugitive, this murdering exiled prince, to bring deliverance.   God uses people we wouldn't use.   God speaks to people we would pass over. Nothing in Moses seems to be leadership material.   He's a quitter. He's a hothead! But, the wilderness has a way of softening a man. It has a way of breaking off the parts that repulse the gentleness of God.

So, when the Lord saw that he turned aside to look, God called to him from the midst of the bush! God uses the broken. He loves the weak and discarded. We are just the refuse of the world. The leftovers. Those who are used up and unworthy of His attention. He sees us and loves us. He wants to touch our brokenness and make us whole. He's looking for that one response.

"Here I am."

Here I am - flow through me.

The bush is a watershed moment for Moses. He will never be the same after this. The presence of God interrupts his routine in the wilderness. It's time. God has perfect timing for the overflow to happen to Moses. He has perfect timing for us.

Moses thought God had forgotten about him. He thought he was off the hook. He was older and not needed. At this time Moses is eighty years old. Most people at eighty are not looking for a leadership position. They are looking for a rocking chair! Moses greatest leadership doesn't begin until this time. He's seasoned. He's wiser. He's not as impetuous. He moves a little slower. He speaks a little softer. He arrives at the burning bush as a broken, older man. Failure is all he has on his resume. What could he do? He is exactly who God is looking for. You are exactly who God is looking for. The overflow of His presence is waiting to pour through you. It's wonderful how in a place that seems so desolate as the wilderness that such life can flow. Where nothing seems to be alive God's presence is moving above the loneliness and simply waiting. He is waiting to move upon the broken. He sees you where you are.

"For the eyes of
the Lord move about on all
the earth to strengthen the
heart that is completely
toward Him."
(2 Chronicles 16:9a MEV)

Nellie and I in Tanzania

Study Guide Questions Chapter 7

Overflow Determines Direction
*Great FOCUS happens in the OVERFLOW
of the Holy Spirit.*

When we lose sight, we can stumble and fall. A greater focus in life comes from seasons of extended fellowship with the Holy Spirit. That fellowship will increase a godly direction.

Matthew 4:1 MEV
"Then Jesus was led up into the wilderness by the Spirit to be tempted by the devil"

James 1:12 NKJV
"Blessed is the man who endures temptation; for when he has been approved, he will receive the crown of life which the Lord has promised to those who love Him."

Have You Been Tempted? What is a Big Temptation?
_____
_____
_____
_____

How Has the Lord Helped You Overcome?
_____
_____
_____
_____

Romans 8:1 NKJV
"There is therefore now no condemnation to those who are in Christ Jesus, who do not walk according to the flesh, but according to the Spirit."

How Has <u>the Overflow of God's Presence</u> Helped You During Temptations or Trials?

_____
_____
_____
_____

Psalm 37:23 NKJV
"The steps of a good man are ordered by the Lord, And He delights in his way."

Even though We Face Trials and Temptations We Know God Still Loves Us. Describe the Difference Between a Trial and a Temptation.

_____
_____
_____
_____
_____
_____
_____

Romans 11:29 NKJV
"For the gifts and the calling of God are irrevocable."

Having Gone Through a Few Trials, How Have You Been Reminded God Still Has His Hand on Your Life?

_____
_____
_____
_____
_____

Romans 8:28 ESV
"And we know that for those who love God all things work together for good, for those who are called according to his purpose."

Installation as Pastor

2001

Pastor Granberry presenting me the Shepherd's Staff

Chapter 8

Splash!

We can ENJOY the OVERFLOW
if we let it OVERFLOW!

"On the last day of the feast, the great day, Jesus stood up and cried out, "If anyone thirsts, let him come to me and drink. [38] Whoever believes in me, as the Scripture has said, 'Out of his heart will flow rivers of living water.'" (John 7:37-38 ESV)

Watching some kids play in the street one day I laughed as I saw them splashing in the puddles. These puddles were the remnants of a flash flood. The laughter and fun were wonderful to witness! What if we were that carefree and full of laughter and joy in the overflow of the Spirit?

That's how our Heavenly Father wants us to rejoice in Him. To laugh and splash in His refreshing overflow.

During the Jewish Feast of Tabernacles there was a Water Celebration Ceremony known as Nissuch Ha-Mayim. It was one of the most popular parts of the celebration of the Feast. One reason the water libation ritual was so popular in Second Temple days was the accompanying ceremony of the water drawing, which took place at night when water was drawn from Siloam for the next morning's water libation. Each day for seven consecutive days the high priest would walk up a ramp leading to the bronze altar located in the Temple Court and pour a vessel full of water into a bowl that drained into the altar.

One of the geographic realities to Israel is the elevation of Jerusalem. The pool of Siloam is low in the valley and the temple altar would have been hundreds of feet higher up on Mount Moriah. Picture the priest lifting the jar from the cool waters and carrying it on his shoulders up the steep steps. God's anointed is careful with every step, not losing a drop of its precious flow. How similar the presence of God is carried on the shoulders of the man of God. Up, up, up the steep steps of prayer and preparation. Not allowing one drop to be spilled. Then in anticipation the congregation waits for the pouring. There at the altar He empties his heart's vessel full of the precious gift. He has dipped into the wells of salvation and there at the altar others find life and build their futures.

The ceremony of the water drawing was a jubilant occasion. The Mishna states, "He that has never seen the joy of the [ceremony of the water drawing] has never in his life seen joy." (Sukkah 51a) As the ceremony took place, Levites played lyres, trumpets, harps, cymbals, and other instruments, while other Levites sang. In the Temple area, three golden candlesticks nearly 75 feet high were lit by young boys climbing tall ladders, and the light from these candlesticks could be seen throughout all Jerusalem. Respected men of faith danced and sang in front of these candlesticks while carrying burning torches. As the ceremony progressed through the night, the priest blew the shofar three times. In the manner of the text, "Therefore, with joy shall ye draw water out of the wells of salvation," (Isaiah 12:3 KJV) the evening was characterized by exuberant joy. It was a wonderful occasion that no one wanted to miss. [1] Sometimes rabbis would perform acrobaticss and juggle flaming torches as part of the festivities. [2]

---

1). This information came from The Feast of Israel, a book written by Bruce Scott who is a Friends of Israel Ministries representative. 2). *Messiah Magazine* # 87 Published through First Fruits of Zion, Devarim 5765 (2005).

Overflow for All!

This is the high point of the festival. He waits for the exact moment He can be heard. One moment earlier and His voice would be extinguished from the noise of the crowd, when the cheering and rejoicing starts to subside. When the crowd just for a moment becomes still and quiet He releases this invitation. Can you hear Him?

"If anyone is thirsty, let him come to Me and drink. Whoever believes in Me, as the Scripture has said, streams of living water will flow from within him." (John 7:37-38)

Picture the faces of the startled worshipers looking at Him. This was not a statement uttered from a closet. This is a bold, direct, unapologetic invitation. It is for all who are thirsty. Thirsty for the presence of God. It is for the exhausted and parched. The desperate are ready! The religious are judging. He declares that He is Messiah. If you want the Holy Spirit, the "living water," not just a jug of it, but a river flowing out of you, then come and drink!

He was saying that He is the one you've been waiting for. The giver of the overflow. The one who can make flow out of you a river of life. Come and drink. Come and enjoy. Splash!

The Blind and the Lame

In 2 Samuel a story is told of when David conquers Jerusalem. "The king and his men marched to Jerusalem to attack the Jebusites, who lived there. The Jebusites said to David, "You will not get in here; <u>even the blind and the lame can ward you off.</u>" They thought, "<u>David cannot get in here</u>." ⁷ Nevertheless, David captured the fortress of Zion—which is the City of David.

⁸ On that day David had said, "Anyone who conquers the Jebusites will have to use the water shaft to reach those 'lame and blind' who are David's enemies." That is why they say, "The 'blind and lame' will not enter the palace." ⁹ David then took up residence in the fortress and called it the City of David. He built up the area around it, from the terraces inward. ¹⁰ And he became more and more powerful, because the Lord God Almighty was with him." (2 Samuel 5:6-10 NIV)

Picture the Jebusites hurling insults at David and his men from this fortress. "We could have the lame and blind guard this city. You'll never get in here! You will never find a way in. You will never be able to reach us." Up until this time no one had conquered the city of Jerusalem. The Jebusites felt secure and safe inside their walls. But every city needs a source of water. Water is the key to survival. With their laughter you can see them leading a blind man to the wall. "Look David, you think you're going to enter here? Haha! You will never! You are foolish, David, if you think you can reach us!" But David did capture the city. He used the water shaft that flowed into what becomes the pool of Siloam. He conquered that fortress and then that fortress became his home. End of story? Not quite.

John Chapter 9

"Now as *Jesus* passed by, He saw a man who was blind from birth. ² And His disciples asked Him, saying, "Rabbi, who sinned, this man or his parents, that he was born blind?" ³ Jesus answered, "Neither this man nor his parents sinned, but that the works of God should be revealed in him. ⁴ I must work the works of Him who sent Me while it is day; *the* night is coming when no one can work. ⁵ As long as I am in the world, I am the light of the world." ⁶ When He had said these things, He spat on the ground and made clay with the saliva; and He anointed the eyes of the blind man with the clay. [7] And He said to him, "Go, wash in the pool of Siloam" (which is translated, Sent). So, he went and washed, and came back seeing. [8] Therefore the neighbors and those who previously had seen that he was blind said, "Is not this he who sat and begged?" [9] Some said, "This is he." Others *said,* "He is like him." He said, "I am *he.*" [10] Therefore they said to him, "How were your eyes opened?" [11] He answered and said, "A Man called Jesus made clay and anointed my eyes and said to me, 'Go to the pool of Siloam and wash.' So, I went and washed, and I received sight." (John 9:1-11 NKJV)

The chapter opens with Jesus *passing by.* When Jesus is passing by, it's time for miracles to begin to happen. When Jesus passes by He's looking for miracles and the miracles are looking for Him. Here He is met by this poor man who has been blind all his life. Imagine the difficulty, the restrictions, the limitations and pain it must have caused him. But the lifter of limitations has just walked into his life. This man has walked in darkness from birth and now the Light of the World has come to him. He lives in the city of Jerusalem.

The creator of the universe once again makes clay and mixes it together with His own spit and forms eyes. He anoints these hollow sockets with the clay and tells the man go wash at the pool of Siloam. The place of the water shaft.

There had to be some excitement as the man asked someone, "Would somebody take me to the pool of Siloam? Can someone lead me? Please hurry! I want to see!" Children take him by the hand and lead him. A crowd of spectators follow along wondering what will happen. With anticipation he enters the pool. A huge crowd has now gathered. Others are saying things like, "the Nazarene put mud in his eyes. Let's see what happens." Many people are pushing and shoving, trying to get a view of the man with the brown, wet dirt smeared across his face. Others are making bets for and against the results.

He splashes down into the pool. He dunks his head and begins to wipe away the mud. There's a pause, then a scream, "I CAN SEE, I CAN SEE!" He says it over and over and then shouts for joy! He splashes around, waving his arms high and begins to praise and worship the Lord! "Thank you, Lord! Thank you, Jehovah God, for sending this man to heal my eyes! Oh, thank you, Almighty Father!" And his praise continues while in amazement the crowd begins to applaud and celebrate with the man. With eyes wide open he looks at his reflection in the water. "I have eyes! I can see!" The people stand in awe and watch the man in amazement as he carefully and slowly walks out of the pool. Dripping with the healing power of Christ flowing from his face, he stands in the warm sunlight and worships. Tears run down his face from eye sockets that just a few minutes ago had nothing. He walks away with no help with clear vision for the very first time.

You may be reading this and you need healing. Maybe it's your eyesight, or something else that seems permanent. Nothing is impossible with Christ. All things are possible! Your impossibility is not the final chapter.

The rest of his life when people look at him, he will say, "I was born blind, a man named Jesus healed me, and gave me these eyes." And just as they asked that day I'm sure throughout his life people continued to ask, "Where is He?" I think He might have said, "Well, He now lives in my heart. I will never forget Him, and I will always remember the day I saw the light of the world." Maybe at some point in the future his grandchild heard the story from his papa. "Papa tell me again how Jesus gave you eyes!"

He tells the story and then gets to the part where he was questioned about who did this. What man? They said, "This man is a sinner!" "He answered and said, "Whether He is a sinner *or not* I do not know. One thing I know: that though I was blind, now I see." (John 9:25 NKJV)

The Blind

David, the blind and the lame will guard this city. You won't be able to get in. You won't conquer it! One thousand years later, Jesus enters the city, and in the same pool and waterway through which David conquers the city, Jesus gives this man his sight. What a wonderful moment! What was conquered with a sword a thousand years before is conquered by Christ by the word of His mouth and the miracle of mud smeared in empty eye sockets.

If Jesus were standing in your church and began to declare with His voice, "If anyone thirsts, let him come to me and drink. 38 Whoever believes in me, as the Scripture has said, 'Out of his heart will flow rivers of living water.'" (John 7:37-38 ESV)

How many people could keep their seats?
How many people would rush …
to the front to be filled?
How many would begin to sob in their thirst?
How many could resist His invitation?
Could you?
Is it possible to reject His appeal?
Is it time for you to respond and say yes?

That river can be yours today. You can splash in the healing waters of heaven's flow. You can be freed from the darkness of this life and receive the light of Christ. Let Him touch your eyes to see this great new life. We were all born into the blindness of this world's sin. We are all needing to have Him anoint our eyes with fresh clay and give us new sight. Heavenly sight that now sees the Son. The light of the world. The true refresher of men's souls.

Thirsty?

God longs to satisfy the thirsty soul. He longs to meet with us. He longs to fill the empty. In John 2, He turns water into wine. In John 3, it's the water of new birth. In John 4, it is the living water offered to the woman at the well. In John 5, it's the cleansing water of Bethesda. In John 6, He calms the waters of life. Then in John 7, He shouts to anyone who is thirsty to come and drink. The day of your spiritual drought is over. God has a message for you. He beckons you to come and drink of the water of life!

Heavenly Refreshing is Available

"And He showed me a pure river of water of life, clear as crystal, proceeding from the throne of God and of the Lamb." (Revelation 22:1 NKJV)

"And the Spirit and the bride say, "Come!" And let him who hears say, "Come!" And let him who thirsts come. Whoever desires, let him take the water of life freely." (Revelation 22:17 NKJV)

Today, Jesus offers this same water to ALL. That powerful water of His presence. Let the overflow of heaven touch you today. Receive Him into your life. Drink. Splash!

"but whoever drinks of the water that I will give him will never be thirsty again. The water that I will give him will become in

him a spring of water welling up to eternal life."
(John 4:14 ESV)

Splash in Your Puddle!

Your place of splashing may not seem as grand as the man healed of his blindness. SPLASH! Splash in your miracle! Enjoy what the Lord has done!

Many times, as we grow up we think someone else has something a little better than we do. Their blessing. Their future seems brighter. Perhaps it is their house, car, spouse, job or life. We can find ourselves being consumed by what others have.

Celebrate the life you have. Celebrate your family. Celebrate friendships and relationships. Enjoy however big or small those puddles are. You may have a family that is huge. Danielle and I are blessed. We have three children by birth and then three by marriage. We presently have ten grandchildren. We are blessed. We have a big family puddle and it is growing every day. I think a lot of times people see someone else's puddle and think *Wow, I bet it would be great to splash over there.*

Then there are those who don't want a puddle. They want a pond or a lake. Their egos are big as an ocean. They are never satisfied with where the Lord has put them and so they are always looking for the bigger and better.

Enjoy this moment. Enjoy this time. One day you may have a bigger puddle and one day it might be a pond or a lake. And then again, you may not, but in the meantime, enjoy your little puddle no matter how big or small.

And "SPLASH!" Splash in that place God has put you.

Dirt Clods

When I wrote "Never Give Up," I retold the story of the season in my life of when it seemed I didn't even have a puddle or a drop. I wanted to quit. It was like my world was dry and if I was lucky I might find a dirt clod. You know dirt clods? Those little clumps of clay and dirt. No water - just a clump of earth.

Yes, it was a dry season. I would have loved a drop of joy, but it seemed it wasn't to be had for a long time.

If life only gives you dirt clods remember, David had only five small, smooth stones, and he brought down a mighty giant. It's not the size of your problem but the size of your God. Jesus turned a couple of dirt clods into eyes. Danielle and I started out in a small Sunday School room doing children's church. I volunteered to help in whatever ministry was needed. Sometimes it seemed I got dirt clods. We were at one time janitors in the church. That church is the one we serve now as lead pastors. We were picking up the dirt clods and other things. We've moved a million tables and chairs and would gladly pick them up today if needed. Some ministries seem like there's not even a pond to splash in. Just like you were getting dirt clods. But all those dirt clods are important.

Splashing in My Puddle

When I was younger I enjoyed my own splash. I couldn't wait for the next big puddle I would be invited to splash in. I would even call my mom and tell her, "Mom you can't believe where I got to minister today." "Mom, I'm at this camp!" "Mom, I'm preaching, a convention!" "Mom, we had 5,000 today at our Easter services!" "Mom, we gave a huge offering in missions today!" Mom would always celebrate with me. Moms and Dads love it when their kids make a big splash!

Danielle and I have had a pool at our house probably for the last ten years. In the summer, we will periodically have our kids and grandkids over to swim. We will grill and enjoy the laughter and the splashing. We cautiously watch our little ones. Those ten grandkids are too special to lose. We keep our eyes on them. It's really awesome when we see them move from just splashing at the edge and then learning to SWIM. They can jump off the edge of the pool and swim across the pool. We celebrate with them each little step they take.

They love to ask me, "Papa, are you getting in?" Sometimes, I'll put on my bathing suit and get in there too. That's a big deal, swimming with Papa and Nana.

Remember, the next generation wants you to SPLASH with them. They need you to celebrate their SPLASH! They need to feel you see them and are excited for their wave.

Waves

When I've gone out and swam with the family sometimes I make my entrance with a big cannonball splash! A cannonball splash is when you double your body up and jump as high as you can and make the biggest splash you can. When you surface you look around and you can see the astonished faces of everyone at your splash. If you caught everyone off-guard they might be upset at the surprise impact. If they were anticipating it they might say, "Wow!" You love looking and seeing the waves are lapping over the edge of the pool. And there's that thump of noise when you hit. It's awesome!

We make waves. I've heard people in a bad situation say, "Don't make waves!" Just as we can make bad waves I believe we can make good waves. Ripples from our lives. When my life is over I pray I've made some waves for Jesus and the gospel. Long after I'm gone, I pray those waves are still pushing out from where I was. My kids are waves from my life. At the 20th little ripple of my life I had a son named Joshua. Another ripple, Michael, came when I was 24 and then a sweet little ripple named Lacey arrived when I was 27. Each of them, have become incredible Christians in their own lives. I'm so proud of them and love them dearly.

I pray they become *TSUNAMIS* for my Savior.

When you see your kids do something that you are so proud of you want to celebrate it. For me I have three pictures of them that I can't get out of my heart. These are pictures of them living in the overflow, watching them making waves.

The first picture is my oldest son Joshua holding and hugging a child in Haiti. What I see on his face is pure, overflowing love. It is powerful. You can see the muscles in his arms. He's tightly holding the little boy. The smile across his mouth is as big as it can get. Everything about the picture is a lesson in love.

SPLASH!

Make Some Waves!

What you fail to really catch at first is that Joshua's son, my first grandchild Caleb, is following right behind his daddy. I've made a wave, Joshua is making a wave and there comes Caleb. I wonder what wonderful waves he will make?

The second picture is of my middle son, Michael. In 2011, 2012 and 2013 we held crusades in India. This picture is of Michael in front of 20-25,000 people at one of our crusade nights. He is ministering a human video drama and he is knocking it out of the park. When I see this, I see him in his element. Where he loves to minister and longs to be reaching the most people. He gets on that stage and he becomes that character in the drama. He is 100% that person and he slams it. He does a dramatic cannonball. He's splashing in a pretty big puddle that night.

Then there's my sweet Lacey, sitting in the dirt in a little slum village in Kenya. She's with three children who are happily watching this young American woman taking time to just play with them. It's a treasure to me. She's this sweet, loving girl giving them time. Giving them attention. She's pushed everything aside for them. In a culture where that is unheard of she is love sitting in the dirt.

I'm so proud of all three of them and I love them with all my heart! Each has a gifting. To one it is one child at a time. To another it is a multitude and to another it is as many as will gather. I would say to all three – SPLASH! Splash with all your might! Make the biggest wave you can for JESUS! What influence will you have on the world? What waves will you make with your lives? I want you to see the world as Jesus sees It. And live your life in the overflow of His love.

Where's your puddle? Where's your pond, lake or ocean? Wherever God has placed you, enjoy and celebrate! Take a big jump and put both feet right in the middle of that puddle and laugh and sing and thank the Lord for His goodness. He placed you in that place for such a time as this.

When we were about to lose everything in 2008-09, I remember going to the church, and calling on God, and I began to celebrate. I really didn't have anything to celebrate, but I knew that He was listening and that He would not turn me away. I just kept asking and kept believing!

Don't give up what little you have. Hold on and never let go. And remember to... make some waves and... *SPLASH!*

Study Guide Questions for Chapter 8

Splash!

We can ENJOY the OVERFLOW
if we let it OVERFLOW!

John 7:37-38 ESV
"On the last day of the feast, the great day, Jesus stood up and cried out, "If anyone thirsts, let him come to me and drink. ³⁸ Whoever believes in me, as the Scripture has said, 'Out of his heart will flow rivers of living water.'"

Watching some kids play in the street one day I laughed as I saw them splashing in the puddles. These puddles were the remnants of a flash flood. The laughter and fun were wonderful! What if we were that carefree and full of laughter and joy in the overflow of the Spirit?

How Have You Enjoyed the Overflow of His Presence? (Describe)

_____
_____
_____
_____
_____

John 9:1 NKJV
"Now as Jesus passed by, He saw a man who was blind from birth."

What is Your Puddle?
Where, Who, When, How...

_____
_____

_____
_____

What Would You <u>Like to See God Do</u> in That?

_____
_____
_____
_____

John 9:25 NKJV
"He answered and said, Whether He is a sinner or not I do not know. One thing I know: that though I was blind, now I see."

What <u>New Areas</u> Would You Like to Reach?

_____
_____
_____
_____
_____

Revelation 22:17 NKJV
"And the Spirit and the bride say, "Come!" And let him who hears say, "Come!" And let him who t
hirsts come. Whoever desires, let him take the water of life freely."

Who Are You Leaving Behind Who Will <u>Make a Wave</u> for Jesus?

_____
_____
_____
_____

Matthew 6:33 MEV
"But seek first the kingdom of God and His righteousness, and all these things shall be given to you."

Andrew, my prayer partner

Chapter 9

Seated in the Overflow

WAITING for Another WAVE of the OVERFLOW!

"Blessed *are* those who have not seen and *yet* have believed."   (John 20:29b NKJV)

I have never enjoyed sitting in the overflow section of an event. You can't feel the emotion of the live performance. You're watching a video, so you might as well have stayed at home. When it comes to church, I am a front-row kind of guy. I like to be there. The closer the better.

When Jesus speaks to Thomas and says, "Blessed are those who have not seen and yet have believed." He's talking about all of us alive today. *We are seated in the overflow.* We weren't present when all this first started. We didn't get to see Christ in person. We didn't get to see His miracles and resurrection. Yet we believe! We know it happened, and Jesus says we are blessed because we believe.

One time, a great couple in our church gave Danielle and me tickets for two very nice seats to a Broadway-type show in Houston. We were excited to go. It was one of those things you do every now and then. We made it a great evening. We were dressed in our best. I had my suit on and she wore a beautiful dress and we went out and had dinner first. The meal was great and then we got to the show. We stood outside with everyone else in the lobby. Finally, the doors opened, and we made our way in. A really nice young man asked to see our tickets. He took us to our seats and we waited for the show to begin. That's when everything changed. After we sat there about ten minutes the young man came back and asked to see our tickets again. He left with them and then came back with an older gentleman, who asked me if he could speak to me. I got up and he quietly told me that we were there on the wrong night. Then he said, "Oh this showing was actually canceled. The night that the people had given us the tickets for this performance wasn't even happening. We were there on a wrong night for a performance that wasn't even happening. We were a little embarrassed. We got up and exited the theater. We could have gone and bought some tickets somewhere I'm sure in the theater, but it had lost its zest. We looked at each other and laughed and said, "Oh my, if these people only knew what just happened they would just die." We laughed and left. It was a crazy evening. Even though we didn't get to see the show we had a great time.

Thinking about that I thought about how you and are seated in the overflow of the Gospel. We were not here when it first showed. Christ came and lived His life and died for our sins and was resurrected long before we got here. We got here late, but there's room for us too. We may be seated in the overflow, but He wants us to know He loves us too.

Frank Leslie Jones and Suzanna "Dollie" Jones Early Pioneer Pentecostal Preachers

"Brother Jones was feeling the call to the ministry, so he sold out..."

"We had A.B. Cox come in off the street, who said he had sinned away his day of grace, he thought, but the Lord got a hold of him at the street meeting that evening and he followed us into the hall and was gloriously saved and filled with the Holy Ghost and made a great preacher."

In Chapter 3 I shared the story of Lucinda Cornelius, my mom's grandmother and how God used her. I was blessed with not just one set of great grandparents who lived in the overflow, but my dad's grandparents were also ministers of the gospel. A few years ago, my uncle David Allard passed onto me a letter that's almost 120 years old now. It tells of the struggles and trials of my great grandparents who were pioneer Pentecostal pastors and the persecution they faced, trying to follow the overflow of God's presence. This letter is written by my great grandmother.

You can understand my wanting to have this letter. I read it today, in this century, in our culture and I think back at what they did. It makes me wonder, *do we have that same pioneering fervor to wait for the overflow of God's presence, today?* Do we want Him enough, that we would wander across states to find His presence? Would we walk and ride in wagons and by horseback to find Him? My prayer is, "Lord help me to wait in your presence to receive the overflow, so I can minister under that same power."

My paternal great grandmother Suzanna "Dollie" Jones holding my grandmother Selma Allard

120 Years Ago

"We received the Holiness experience in 1901, that is, I did. Brother Jones had received it in 1900 under Brother and Sister Cagle at his hometown – Liberty Hills, Texas. Then in 1901 a Brother George Sutton came to my neighborhood schoolhouse and held a meeting and our family, the Albert Lohmann family all embraced holiness and was put out of the Methodist church. We began services of our own, there in the schoolhouse, and continued on until we married December 24th, 1903. We lived in the Jones' home the first year of our married life and he made a crop on the place-him being the last boy to marry of the family. After the crop was gathered, we moved to my fathers for a month until after our first child was born, then we moved to Liberty Hill for a month.

He then rented a farm 7 or 8 miles west of town. We wintered there and went to church at Bertram to the Holiness Tabernacle there where Brother Jim Manney was Pastor. Brother Jones was feeling the call to the ministry, so he sold out the crop he had started, and we loaded our wagon and headed for Peniel, Texas to go to school to study for the ministry, but we failed to go to Peniel. We went to Lampasas and got in a meeting there with Brother Manney. Got acquainted with another young holiness preacher by the name of Phelps, so they asked us into their home. So, one day the young wife was forced to leave him by her mother and taken away, so he gave up his job and he and Brother Jones accepted a traveling job with a sewing machine co. We loaded up the sewing machines and left out, they thought to sell sewing machines. We traveled one day and sold nothing, so night was coming on and we couldn't get back to Lampasas so we just pitched camp on the river. Next morning, they headed back and gave up the job. We loaded our wagon and left out thinking we would go to Peniel but instead we traveled over bad roads and slept out beside the wagon for a number of days and nights until we came to Grapevine, Texas. Where he had a cousin John Jones who lost his wife. We stayed there for a week or so, then went on over into Oklahoma.

Crossing the river at Gainesville where the quick sands were, was so bad you didn't dare let the horses stop or they would sink. The men who guided us over tied their horses to the bridles of our horses and told Brother Jones to lay the whip on them. I was scared half to death. They carried us in a high lope all the way over.

Then when we got over we ran into the cross timbers and sand roughs. No roads to speak of. Ran into a place so narrow one of our wagon bows was broken, so we had to get out and chop trees out of the way before we could go on, so I told him we surely must be on the wrong road – we saw a man plowing in a small field. Stopped and asked him the directions out to the place we were supposed to go to find the river. Then we were scared the man might follow us and try to rob us, so we drove hard as we could until we met a bad cloud coming up, had to pull the wagon off the road to get a place to camp. I got up a few sticks of wood and put them under the wagon, so we could build a fire the next morning. He tied the horses close by and fed them. By the time the cloud had struck and such a storm looked as if it would blow us away. We really did pray. As soon as day began to dawn he got out and built a fire and fed the team and the coyotes began to yell right close to the camp. I was really glad to see daylight again.

We finally made it to Duncan, Oklahoma. Where he had a sister living. Stayed there for a while, and one of our horses got shot and killed there. So, we had to trade the wagon for a horse back. Then we went from there to Oklahoma City, that fall of 1904. Went into the orphanage and did rescue work there with Matty Mallory and Richard Bell. Stayed there until the fall of 1906. Left there and went back to Duncan after our second baby died September 1, 1906.

Stayed at Duncan until Christmas and Brother Jones left me and the little girl Selma and went to Putnam, Oklahoma. Then I followed him after he got us a place to live. It was there we heard of the Holy Ghost Baptism. A young boy had been where people received the Holy Ghost and told us about it. Then Brother Jones went to Oklahoma City for the camp meeting of the holiness people. There he saw the people who had received it and heard them speak in tongues. Saw the main men of the Holiness movement fight it yet Dr. Godfey who spoke 17 different languages understood 5 different languages – that a young girl spoke while prostrate under the power of God. Brother Richard Bell our fellow worker in the Rescue work had already received it so Brother Jones accepted in his heart then and came home and told me, so I said, "well, I'll believe it for I read it in the Bible."

We began seeking for it the best we knew. I believe I would have received it then if I had obeyed what I felt to do but was backward and timid, so I didn't do what I felt I was moved upon to have the Brother who was with us in a meeting to lay hands on me. During that meeting a Brother C.M. Packer came and gave his experience. At the close of the meeting we went back to Oklahoma City to start back to school at the holiness college. The principal told the students that if any of them went downtown to the mission they were automatically out of the school.

So, one day at noon he told me to have the babies ready when he got out of school, that we were going down to the mission. So, we did, that was Friday P.M. We both received the Holy Ghost before returning Sunday night. From there we moved into the mission building up over-head. We had a marvelous something of the Supernatural to take place there one night after the service closed. We had all gone to bed. There was 6 of we adults and the 2 babies living up there. The fire whistle blew, and it blew our ward and we heard the fire wagons coming right down our street and pulled around into the alley. So, we all jumped out of bed and ran to the back to see. So, there was huge pillar of fire just standing over our building and between the big building next to ours. We had many supernatural things to take place there such as balls of fire and smoke of incense was seen by different people.

One night we had a young lady to come off the street and rushed to the altar, crying out to God. She was one of the girls from the holiness college and was on her way to the river to commit suicide. She was wonderfully saved, and I believe she received the Baptism. We had A.B. Cox come in off the street, who said he had sinned away his day of grace, he thought, but the Lord got a hold of him at the street meeting that evening and he followed us into the hall and was gloriously saved and filled with the Holy Ghost and made a great preacher. He is one of the Assembly of God ministers up in Ohio.

From Oklahoma City we went to what is now Carter, Oklahoma. It was then called Beulah. There we went through the first Holy Ghost school in Oklahoma where Brother Frank T. Alexander was the founder of the school. Brother Daniel Awery was the Bible leader. Brother R.E. Winsett was music teacher. Sister Birdie Bell who later became Brother Winsett's wife was one of the primary teachers.

There was both literary and Bible classes. There was more than 40 of us there and everyone had to trust God for our support and we never did lack a meal, only when fast days arrived. We saw God move in a great way in supplying the need of the school — financially and physically. We had some serious sickness among the people and God came to our rescue and healed every one of them.

Brother Awery and his wife were people of faith. They trusted God for everything. He left at the close of school and went around the world. When he kissed his family good-bye he had 30 cents in his pocket, but God had spoken to him to go, so he told his wife to pack his grip, which she did. The brothers at the school took him to the depot and he boarded the train. God always put it in someone's heart and mind to give him a certain amount of money before the conductors would get around to punch tickets.

I've seen him receive letters from people who didn't even know him and say the Lord has spoken to me to send you a certain amount of money and gave them his name and address, and always it would be at a time when we were in need at the school.

At the close of the school we were all sent out in bands to hold meetings over the country. Everywhere we went there was a goodly number received the Holy Ghost. One of the places a band of us went was Cordell, Oklahoma. There is where

Brother Jones tells us about getting his whipping with the rawhide buggy whip.

We had a lot of persecution there. They cut our tent ropes, so the men had to just stay out and watch and tie them back all the time. The gang would ride by on horses and curse and shoot their guns and one night hollered to us if we lit the lights the next night they would shoot them out. So, the next morning Brother Alexander who was our leader, called us all together and told us that we were going to have to do something and told us all to go to praying alone. No 2 of us together. So, we scattered all over the farm to pray and God spoke to everyone to put it in His hands, so that was what we did.

During the song service some fellows slipped up and cut one of the little ropes. Sister Hill and I were sitting just outside of the tent by their wagon. They were camped on the grounds and we saw this man when he cut the rope. When the song service was over Brother Alexander made the announcement that we had put everything in the hands of God; and for them to cut all the ropes that God would let them cut; throw all the rocks God would let them throw and shoot all the bullets that God would let them shoot. So, everything got so still you could of heard a pin drop and the fellow who cut the rope slipped up and tied it back again.

The next day or so the power fell, and the persecution began sure enough. A young lady, the ring leader of the young people of the county fell in the altar and was saved and filled with the Holy Ghost in the day service. So, her brother-in-law got stirred and got hold of her father and had him all stirred up. During the night service his other daughter was in the altar and had fallen under the power, so the daddy tried to get her out, pulled her up and she couldn't stand. By the time the Lord had took hold of him and tried to get her sister to take her, she threw her arms up and praised God, so the daddy just began to holler and preach to the crowd: "tell them it was God and not to fight it but come and receive it."

The brother-in-law let the devil take him. He is the man Brother Jones tells about coming to the house where Brother Alexandeand us stayed that night and tried to kill Brother Alexander. Brother Alexander never tried to get away from him. Just stood still and talked to the man and told him what would happen to him, so in less than 4 months he died a raving maniac.

That winter of 1908, we went into Houston, Texas for the Bible school there. At the close of the school in the spring of 1909 we were sent to Austin, Texas to work there. From there we went to Brother Jones' home town, Liberty Hill, Texas and pitched a tent meeting there after quite a lot of opposition."

Dollie

Note:
(Papa Jones won A.B. Cox to the Lord. A.B. Cox won J.W. Welch and brought him to Pentecost in 1910. J.W. Welch became a General Superintendent of the Assemblies of God. A.B. Cox also held meetings with Aimee Semple McPherson in 1920 at his church Bethel Temple in Dayton, Ohio. There were 100,000 in estimated attendance in the meetings. It is also estimated over 5,000 were anointed for healing and there were over 1,000 converts. A.B Cox also established 17 churches and 73 full-time ministers came from his ministry.)

In April 1914, Frank and Suzanna "Dollie" Jones attended a meeting with 300 other hungry hearts, in Hot Springs, Arkansas. They were waiting in the overflow for all that the Father had. They gathered there, and in that meeting, which would become the beginning of what is now the largest Pentecostal denomination in the world, with over 75 million adherents, the Assemblies of God. Its mission, since its inception, has been to take the gospel, to the uttermost parts of the world. They were a part of that humble beginning.

Formation meeting of the Assemblies of God, Hot Springs, Arkansas, April 1914

Years ago, when Danielle and I were just starting out in the ministry, she used to sing a song, "Ordinary People." There's a lyric in that song that says, "God uses ordinary people." I believe that. Papa and Granny were just ordinary people. Yet because of the overflow of God's presence in their lives, they became extraordinary. They were willing to leave everything to follow Him. Even to the ends of the earth. They trusted Him all their lives. They lived in the overflow of His love and shared it with everyone. Their journey took them through hard trials and persecutions. At one time, papa was tied to a tree and whipped with a buggy whip and told "Don't come back with that nonsense." He preached the truth, he preached hell hot and heaven free to all who would believe in Jesus. He never saw Jesus in this life, yet he believed. Granny was the same, and yet she believed. They were seated in the overflow and heard about a Savior. How wonderful, how marvelous this amazing story of grace!

A Few Things I Learned from Them

1. **Give it All You've Got**
2. **My Life is Not My Own**
3. **Never Look Back**

In a way I feel like I'm a part of being in the overflow because of what flowed out of them. I know they loved the Lord with their whole heart. When I read of their sacrifice and commitment I ask myself am I willing to do the same?

Let's invite all the people we can to be seated with us in the overflow. One day, our sweet precious Savior will come back for us. He will step through the door of heaven and invite us to the front, to see all of it for ourselves. We will celebrate with all of those who were there at the beginning. No longer a mystery but it will be clear, because we will see Him face to face.

Jesus said,

"I am the vine, you are the branches. He who abides in Me, and I in him, bears much fruit; for without Me you can do nothing." (John 15:5 NKJV)

I'm glad I was invited to sit in the overflow and hear the same amazing story. I have not been disappointed. It has been wonderful to see the faces of people I've invited to sit with me. They too have invited others to join us in the overflow. It is never too crowded and there is always room for more. We're saving you a seat. *Come join us...*

Seated in the Overflow!

"Therefore, we also, since we are surrounded by so great a cloud of witnesses, let us lay aside every weight, and the sin which so easily ensnares *us,* and let us run with endurance the race that is set before us." (Hebrews 12:1 NKJV)

Study Guide Questions for Chapter 9

Seated in the Overflow
WAITING for Another WAVE
of the OVERFLOW!

John 20:29b NKJV
"Blessed are those who have not seen and yet have Believed."

I have never enjoyed sitting in the overflow section of an event. You can't feel the emotion of the live performance. You're watching a video, so you might as well have stayed home. When it comes to church, I am a front-row kind of guy. I like to be there. The closer the better.

What Distracts You in the Overflow?

_____
_____
_____
_____

How Has God Blessed You Because of the Previous Generations?

_____
_____
_____
_____
_____

Hebrews 12:1 NKJV
"Therefore, we also, since we are surrounded by so great a cloud of witnesses, let us lay aside every weight, and the sin which so easily ensnares us, and let us run with endurance the race that is set before us."

John 15:5 NKJV
"I am the vine, you are the branches. He who abides in Me, and I in him, bears much fruit; for without Me you can do nothing."

What Do You Think the People in Heaven Are <u>Cheering</u> as They Watch You?

_____
_____
_____
_____
_____

What Do You Think the <u>Next Wave</u> of God's Overflow Will Look Like?

_____
_____
_____
_____
_____

<u>How</u> Should We Pray For that Overflow?

_____
_____
_____
_____
_____

Matthew 20:16 NKJV
"So, the last will be first, and the first last. For many are called, but few chosen."

What Does that Verse Mean to You?

_____
_____
_____
_____
_____

Psalm 96:1 NKJV

"Oh, sing to the Lord a new song! Sing to the Lord, all the earth."

My son Joshua worshiping at the Sea of Galilee

Chapter 10

What's Holding You Back?

No Apologies Needed for a
LIFE that OVERFLOWS!

"Then He said to them, "The harvest truly *is* great, but the laborers *are* few; therefore, pray the Lord of the harvest to send out laborers into His harvest. (Luke 10:2 NKJV)

Remember in Chapter 5 when I spoke about the trip to Israel in 2012. The trip of our own design? On that trip the second-to-the-last day I met a very special man, a man who would become a dear friend, Dr. Alon Barak. We had been hoping to get on a boat at the Sea of Galilee but had no clue most are booked way in advance. As he was getting off a boat and I was getting on, we passed by each other and engaged in casual conversation. For some reason, our friendship just took off from there. I'm really not sure who spoke first (it was probably him) but it started, I think, with him asking what we were doing in the land. I responded that we were just looking at the holy sites. He then mentioned about seeing sites that you don't see on a normal tour. From there, we were all in. He started talking about the Yeshua Triangle, the area where Jesus did most of His ministry. And how Dr. Alon spoke of how Jesus had ministered in all the Galilean synagogues. It was a timely and wonderful meeting. The next day we spent in Galilee together. We did a one-day tour with Dr. Alon and it was great.

In 2013 I came back for a few weeks' sabbatical. It was May, and I had timed my visit to land on the holiday of Pentecost. I had always celebrated Pentecost in America with whatever church we were a part of. But this was different. We were there. This was fantastic. We were able to go to Jerusalem and see the celebrating and prayers at the wall. It was wonderful. Shofars blowing, praying, shouting, singing, dancing; it was amazing! If you can ever schedule a time to be in Jerusalem during Pentecost, please do so.

We planned a special day of sightseeing on the day of Pentecost. When would I ever be there again, on this day? What should we see first? Where should we end our tour? I couldn't think of anything better than starting the morning in the upper room, on Mount Zion. This is the traditional place believed to be site of the initial outpouring of the Holy Spirit baptism and birth of the church. It was surreal thinking about the day and what it meant.

"When the day of Pentecost had come, they were all together in one place. [2] Suddenly a sound like a mighty rushing wind came from heaven, and it filled the whole house where they were sitting. [3] There appeared to them tongues as of fire, being distributed and resting on each of them, [4] and they were all filled with the Holy Spirit and began to speak in other tongues, as the Spirit enabled them to speak." (Acts 2:1-4 MEV)

The original building is no longer there. What now exists is a crusader-era building that has stood the test of time. It is such a powerful place to think on Mount Zion that the precious Holy Spirit descended on that very spot. The 120 disciples gathered in that room waiting for the overflow of heaven. They had no idea what they were going to receive; they only knew that Jesus had said go and wait.

"Being assembled with them, He commanded them, "Do not depart from Jerusalem, but wait for the promise of the Father, of which you have heard from Me. [5] For John baptized with water, but you shall be baptized with the Holy Spirit not many days from now." (Acts 1:4-5 MEV)

I could just picture the ten days of waiting from the ascension to the time of the fullness of the blessing. Just like my Grandmother Cornelius worshiped in a barn and received the baptism while milking a cow, they were worshiping in this upper room, waiting and praying for this new overflow from heaven. They were believing for the promise of the Father to fall fresh. It had to be wonderful. Then suddenly a rushing, powerful wind began to blow, and something they had never felt before began to fill every one of them. Fiery tongues appeared on each believer. They all began to speak in other tongues as the Spirit gave them an utterance. It surely was powerful. The church was born that day. The worship and the prayer meeting poured over into the streets.

People visiting from other nations were hearing the worship and prayers in their languages. The outsiders began to question what was going on. Then, the apostle Peter brings the outpouring to a point of connection with the crowd and begins to preach. Three thousand new believers were added to the church that day. This was the overflow of heaven coming to mankind. This is the overflow of Pentecost!

Oh God please give us an overflow like that again! When we push back agendas and schedules and stay in your presence. What would happen if we shut ourselves in the Father's house for ten days? What would happen if we said no to all outside interference and said we are waiting until? Until God visits us with His precious presence!

What would happen to all of us? We would have a heavenly visit of the Lord's presence. It would overflow our building and it would pour into our businesses, schools, homes, and every area of our life, and nothing would ever be the same.

I wasn't alone on this sabbatical. My son Michael and I were there with Dr. Alon and a great friend, Kevin Fisher. It was awesome! Every step and every day was filled with something new.

Many Christians have never heard of the Jewish tradition that Kind David was born on the day of Pentecost, and that he also died on the day of Pentecost. Yet another tradition is that King David is buried on Mount Zion, and his tomb is directly under the area of the upper room. Let that sink in a moment. So, I'm at the upper room, on the day of Pentecost and it's also the birthday of King David and the anniversary day of his death. It's a King David kind of day. But my mind rushed back to the upper room and the significance of those early disciples. What Jesus had told them to do... What He tells all of us to do...

Wait!

What if Jesus told you to wait? What if He said I have a package being delivered to your house? It should be arriving any day. His instructions are for you not to leave until you receive it. It's going to be very special. It will change your life. It'll be just like you have Him with you all the time when you receive this gift. How many of us would think of an excuse or a few excuses or a dozen valid reasons why we need to leave, before the delivery of that package?

How many altar times are cut short by schedules? How many prayer meetings stop at a set time? I'm just as bad as the next pastor, trying to keep things moving along. Of course, you may have multiple services. My church does and we try to be conscious of everyone's time, but there are days all the schedules go out the window and we just linger and wait. And the next service finds the first service still there and the Holy Spirit is being poured out on everyone. Just like that day 2,000 years ago.

Jesus said, "Wait!"

Can't you wait for Jesus?" Can't you wait a few days to receive this special gift? This gift is like no other. You will be completely different. He wants to send His overflow into your life!

When the presence of the Holy Spirit finally descends upon the crowd it was on the day of Pentecost. This is the same day God had sent the Torah on Mount Sinai. So, Jerusalem is packed with people there to celebrate Shavout, Pentecost. The feast of weeks. This is the same day God delivers to Moses the law. On the exact same day with fire on the mountain and there in the New Testament the fire on the mountain is the day of Pentecost on Mount Zion. One was for the law of Moses, and one was for the way of Christ. Powerful, all on the day of Pentecost.

Following the visit to the upper room we made our way to the tomb of King David downstairs. We are deeply humbled that we are there at the location of his burial, and at the spot where the church is born. I thought of all the wonderful Psalms David wrote. Of his battles, struggles, failures and triumphs. A man after God's own heart. He was the sweet singer of Israel. The shepherd boy who becomes king. A powerful story, to say the least. I have often thought how insignificant I was as a boy. I shouldn't be where I am today, leading this wonderful church.

The world would have considered me a nobody. I didn't have a lot going for me. But Jesus raises up the insignificant. He uses the weak things. The castaway and orphan are His. You may feel like that. *Like what could I ever do for God? I'm a nobody.* Listen, the devil will lie and tell you that you are a nobody, but Christ has made us more than conquerors. He has set us apart as vessels and instruments to be used in His hand. What a joy to serve the Lord!

Defeating Giants

Where will our third stop be? Where should we go next? On this very special David kind of day. Only one place I can think of. It's one of my all-time favorite stories in the Bible, and it's found in 1 Samuel 17.

"And Saul and the men of Israel were gathered together, and they encamped in the Valley of Elah, and drew up in battle array against the Philistines. [3] The Philistines stood on a mountain on one side, and Israel stood on a mountain on the other side, with a valley between them. [4] And a champion went out from the camp of the Philistines, named Goliath, from Gath, whose height *was* six cubits and a span." (1 Samuel 17:2-4 NKJV)

This would be a day I would always remember. It will be a day filled with an overflow of good memories. With memories that are filled with God and His goodness to me. This would be a day I would stand in footsteps of David.

"Moreover, David said, "The Lord, who delivered me from the paw of the lion and from the paw of the bear, He will deliver me from the hand of this Philistine." (1 Samuel 17:37 NKJV)

To stand there in that field and see the place and dream of what it must have felt like for that young boy facing that warrior. He doesn't back up or back down. He charges the giant. He speaks with courage and has this unwavering trust in the Lord. I'm not sure what giants you are facing. I don't know what battlefield you find yourself on today. Maybe it's the battlefield of cancer, or depression.   Maybe you're overwhelmed with loneliness or desperate for a financial matter to change. There's a promise from God's word like a pebble you can take up today. Don't quit. Don't give up the fight. Declare the promises of God. Speak LIFE over the need. *Never Give Up!*

"Then he took his staff in his hand; and he chose for himself five smooth stones from the brook, and put them in a shepherd's bag, in a pouch which he had, and his sling was in his hand. And he drew near to the Philistine." (1 Samuel 17:40 NKJV)

With Five Smooth Stones and His Faith in God, David Drew Near to Fight the Giant of Gath!

Dr Alon Barak and I standing in that dry creek bed,
both holding five smooth stones each.

Stepping Out in Faith

As I sit here today writing about the overflow, thinking of David's valiant fight with Goliath, I'm dealing with a giant feeling in my own heart. It's a little overwhelming. Feeling somewhat down. Yes, even pastors have days like that. It seems as I'm writing and coming to an end of writing that the enemy has really reared his head.

How many times have you stepped out in faith believing for something and it seems the opposite of what you needed to see started happening. I'm dreaming and believing today for the future expansion of our children's area at the church and I'm needing to see the blessing with my eyes, but giving has taken a dip at the church. We are doing everything we've been doing for years now. Faithfully giving hundreds of thousands of dollars in missions. We have given millions over the past two years to missions, in fact. In one week, I will celebrate ten years faithfully coming to early morning prayer at the church. If I'm in town, Monday through Friday, I'm here at 5:30 or 6 a.m., at the church praying with my team. Yet today, I find Crossroads in need. We're needing a turnaround in finances. It looks like a giant, but I know God is able to do this. God has abundance for our church. He has abundance for you and your need. He wants to bless you with His overflow. Even when you are doing what you're supposed to do you can find yourself at a test. I feel today like I'm in a test. Maybe it's to help me write this part of the book with an anointing to help someone who will read this. Even when sometimes you are doing everything you are supposed to do you can face major challenges. Don't quit!

This morning, I'm sitting in the sanctuary that we were once unable to finish because we were broke. It was literally IMPOSSIBLE! I look around at all that God has done. God did come through. We did experience a miracle, and you will too. This was my Valley of Elah. Goliath was defeated here. He lost his head here. And now, week after week I preach from this platform the greatness of Almighty God. What a great, good God I serve. I am so honored to pastor this church.

July 16, 2013
Pouring the foundation for the platform
In the main sanctuary at Crossroads Fellowship

A few months after that trip to Israel and the day of Pentecost that I spent remembering David and his struggles. I came home with a bag of small, smooth stones from the Valley of Elah. I mean I had a suitcase of small, smooth stones. I remember giving those stones to a lot of people. You may have even received one. Tuesday, July 16, 2013, was five years to the day that we had poured the slab for the main foundation of the church. Five years we had waited and waited to build that sanctuary out. It was in every sense of the word impossible. It was a giant to us. But this day was a day of victory. I took a new Bible and five smooth stones from the Valley of Elah and laid them in the grid of that new platform. Then when the concrete was poured those five smooth stones and that Bible were forever embedded into the church platform. My declaration from that day to this day, and beyond was that this church would be built on the word of God and that we would raise up *GIANT KILLERS* for the Lord!

The Word of God

Those stones and Bible are there under my feet every week that I preach. I believe every week "God, destroy the giants that are trying to destroy your people. Raise up a next generation that will defeat the enemy and win the battle."

As you read this let the Holy Spirit overflow your soul. Remember all that God has done to bring you to this place. Remember the days and nights Christ spent in prayer. Think of the wilderness and the desert He walked through. He carries today your grief and your sorrow. He hasn't forgotten you on the field of battle. He hasn't left you to fight the giant by yourself.

"Lift up your heads, O you gates!
And be lifted up, you everlasting doors!
And the King of glory shall come in.
[8] Who *is* this King of glory?
The Lord strong and mighty,
The Lord mighty in battle.
[9] Lift up your heads, O you gates!
Lift up, you everlasting doors!
And the King of glory shall come in.
[10] Who is this King of glory?
The Lord of hosts,
He *is* the King of glory. *Selah"*

(Psalm 24:7-10 NKJV)

The word "SELAH" means to "THINK ON THIS." So, think on this. Let it overflow your soul!

He is the King of glory. He knows exactly where you are. He wants to bless and pour out His Spirit on you today. Let Him give you your own personal day of Pentecost. Allow Him to overflow your soul with His refreshing. Let Him help you in the battle. Let Him empower you to defeat every weapon Satan would try to bring against you to harm you.

Let the King of glory help you today destroy the doubt and fear that tries to bring destruction. Let Him lift you out of the place that feels so dark. He is strong and mighty. He is the Lord mighty in battle.

Before we left the Valley of Elah I couldn't help but notice the field of wheat we were standing in. The field we stood in was covered waist-high with the golden grain ready to be harvested. I told the guys, "Look at this field of grain! The grain is ready, it is ready to be harvested!" It was literally falling off the stems. The grain fell to the ground as we brushed through it. The little pieces seemed to get lost in the sea of gold. The precious harvest was ready. It made me think of what Jesus said in Luke 10.

"Then He said to them, the harvest truly *is* great, but the laborers *are* few; therefore, pray the Lord of the harvest to send out laborers into His harvest. (Luke 10:2 NKJV)

We walked back to the car and headed out to our next stop that day. I looked back and thanked the Lord that He was my Savior and that He had made this day so special for me. I thought about all the battles He's brought me through. And nothing has been too hard for the Lord.

Our final stop was a place I hadn't seen in thirty-three years. When I was just twenty years old I took my first trip to Israel, a trip that I received as a gift. The first church we had served as youth pastors was the church I served with my father-in-law Dan Heil. The church gave a trip to Israel to my in-laws and my mother-in-law had said she didn't want to go. She doesn't like to travel. This opened up a spot for someone. Well, Pastor Heil asked me to go in her place. For that I will always be grateful to my sweet mother-in-law. She's a jewel.

"Then David went up from there and dwelt in strongholds at Ein Gedi." (1 Samuel 23:29 NKJV)

Among the beautiful things in Ein Gedi are the waterfalls. They cascade from pool to pool. There in the desert wilderness of Negev just a few miles from the Dead Sea is this oasis. It's lush, and the mountain caves offer a great place to hide from your enemies. The mountain Ibex offer a bounty of fresh meat for the others who would find shelter with David there. This is David's hideout. I couldn't believe I was back. It was greener to me than it was three decades before. It was beautiful. The fresh mountain spring water crashed down on the ground forming a beautiful pool of crisp, clear water.

I could just see that young warrior coming to the water and dipping his hands in to get a drink. Looking around and filling his canteen skin for his journey. Sweat dripping from his face and feeling the refreshing, cool blessing on his head as he splashes it on his face.

The young shepherd boy has gotten older. He's had to become wiser. His arms have become scarred from battles. He never dreamed that when the prophet came to his home and anointed him that day, so much would change. The simple

The waterfalls at Ein Gedi

sheepherder was now a fugitive. He was on the king's most wanted list to capture. No, he was no longer a shepherd boy. He was a man on the run. Ein Gedi was a perfect hideout. It gave protection from the heat and it provided a bounty of good food. And yet, He had often thought of that day the prophet Samuel came, and asked David's father Jesse to call all his sons together.

Anointing

"Then Samuel took the horn of oil and anointed him in the midst of his brothers; and the Spirit of the Lord came upon David from that day forward..." (1 Samuel 16:13 NKJV)

David thinks back to that special day when life was simple. When waking up to the sounds of the farm and the smells of the land were everywhere. How he enjoyed holding the lambs. How he would sing while watching the clouds roll by, but not anymore. David is the one man that King Saul wants gone!

David loves the Lord more than anything and desires to please him. That's why he's known as a man after God's own heart. His heart literally chases after the Lord. So, the Spirit of the Lord rests on him. He not only drinks from this spring but he drinks from the spring of his Heavenly Father. He reflects and sits and stares into the water. Then he lays back in the grass and remembers the shepherd's fields near Bethlehem. An old psalm comes to his mind as he worships.

"Surely goodness and mercy shall follow me All the days of my life; And I will dwell in the house of the Lord Forever." (Psalm 23:6 NKJV)

I sat there and looked around and wondered what David felt. What emotions must he have felt when he finds his king was now against him? The king wants him dead. How does he survive this? How does he go forward? How will he pull himself up and remind himself that God's goodness and mercy are his, and that he would dwell in the house of the Lord forever?

This was David's place to retreat and refresh himself. We all need that. We all need an Ein Gedi. We need the overflow of the waterfall of God's blessings coming down on us. We need to feel He hasn't forgotten us. Every once in a while we feel a little sad and lonely, but it soon leaves when we come into His presence and we renew our spirit. How many times do we fail to remember that? How many times do we run on our own strength? Like a stray lamb. Seeing how far away it can wander before the shepherd brings it back. Day by day we learn to trust in the Lord. We overflow with His love.

High Places

As the day started to draw to a close we were headed back to the car and we began to notice something high up on the clifts. It was the ibex. The Bible calls them "hinds or deer" There were dozens and dozens. It looked like a heard of fifty or more. I was shocked to see so many. They were almost dancing on a vertical cliff wall high up. Jumping effortlessly to the next rock. Sometimes they paused for just a moment, then they would jump and run. It looked impossible, but they were doing it.

"He makes my feet like the *feet* of deer, And sets me on my high places." (2 Samuel 22:34 NKJV)

"He makes my feet like the *feet of* deer, And sets me on my high places." (Psalm 18:33 NKJV)

Living in the Overflow!

I can see David in his later years. Sitting in a field. Maybe he's down near a stream and he looks up and he sees the ibex jumping from rock to rock. His heart is moved as he remembers the caves of Ein Gedi. He remembers the desert wilderness. How he longed for his home. How he saw the deer jumping and leaping from rock to rock. His hair is now gray. His face has lines. His movement is not as swift as it once was. His eyes still weep when he thinks of God's goodness. He smiles as he watches them jump.

Psalm 18 opens with this preamble...

"To the Chief Musician. A Psalm of David the servant of the Lord, who spoke to the Lord the words of this song on the day that the Lord delivered him from the hand of all his enemies and from the hand of Saul. And he said:" (Psalm 18:1 NKJV)

"For who *is* God, except the Lord?
And who *is* a rock, except our God?
32 *It is* God who arms me with strength,
And makes my way perfect.
33 He makes my feet like the *feet of* deer,
And sets me on my high places."
(Psalm 18:31-33 NKJV)

Let Him set you on a high place today. Let the Lord make your feet swift like the feet of deer. Run and let Him do great things through your life.

The day of Pentecost 2013 was a great and refreshing day. I got to enjoy it with one of my sons and two other great friends. It was a day I'll never forget. From the upper room, to the battlefield of Elah and the waterfalls of Ein Gedi. It was a blessed day. A day that overflowed and still does in my heart.

My memory is still overflowing from that day of God's delivering goodness.

You see when I went on that sabbatical in 2013 I was leaving the US with the knowledge that the Crossroad's sanctuary was being completed. The battle for that was behind me. It was a giant that had almost defeated me, but it was powerless. I could rest in the Lord and think of His goodness.

But one triumphant battle, even though it is a great one, is not the ending. We must continue. We can't let one fight be the end of the journey. As hard as some of our journeys are it is not over until we hear the Master say, "Well done my good and faithful servant." So, we fight on. We live in the overflow. We splash in the blessings of the Lord. And we take our seat in the overflow and we await His return. What a great day that will be.

So, what's holding you back?

Ibex of Ein Gedi

Study Guide Questions for Chapter 10
What's Holding You Back?
No Apologies Needed for a
LIFE that OVERFLOWS!

Luke 10:2 NKJV
"Then He said to them, "The harvest truly is great, but the laborers are few; therefore, pray the Lord of the harvest to send out laborers into His harvest."

In Chapter 5, I spoke about the trip to Israel in 2012. It was the trip of our own design, and on that trip the second to the last day, I met a very special man, a man who would become a dear friend, Dr. Alon Barak.

Sometimes Living in the Overflow Will Cause You to <u>Meet Unexpected People</u>. Name an Encounter that has Changed You.

_____
_____
_____
_____
_____

What Could Be a Reason <u>Why</u> the Early Disciples Needed the Ten Days to Wait for the Promise of the Holy Spirit to Come?

_____
_____
_____
_____
_____
_____

Name a Giant or Two that <u>You've Seen God Defeat</u> in Your Life.

_____
_____
_____
_____
_____

What's a Giant You're Facing Right Now?

_____
_____
_____
_____

What's an Area In Which You've <u>Stepped Out in Faith</u> and What's an Area Where You Know <u>You Need to?</u>

_____
_____
_____
_____
_____
_____
_____
_____

Duane and Fasaji

Fasaji is a Haitian grandmother Duane witnessed to for years.

Chapter 11

Creating a Tsunami of Love!

Every Action Has a Reaction!

"His lord said to him, 'Well *done,* good and faithful servant; you were faithful over a few things, I will make you ruler over many things. Enter into the joy of your lord.'"
(Matthew 25:21 NKJV)

Every action has an equal and opposite reaction. Newton's law of motion explains that physical law has a relationship with all mechanical actions. In essence all energy of force and motion will have an equal and reverse energy of force and motion. The same can be said for actions of love and giving. When I give and let love overflow from my life it can have a huge impact on the life of someone else. It's like watching dominoes fall. One triggers a line and before you know it, they are all falling over because of the effect of one. One domino moves the rest. That's how the momentum of love affects others.

The word tsunami comes from two Japanese words. They are tsu meaning "harbor" and nami meaning "wave." The immediate information on social media has boosted the reality of how terrible these monster events really are. They are the result of earthquakes and the movement of tectonic plates of the earth's crust shifting. We see massive waves of water and flows of mud destroying whole towns. Houses are uprooted by the force of the waves. Immense damage happens in the wake of the tsunami. Startled villagers gaze in amazement as the water rushes away into the sea only to return with such torrential power that everything is destroyed in its wake.

The antithesis of a tsunami of destruction is a tsunami of love. Every day I hear of people God are using around the world to touch the nations for Christ. Hidden in far-off places, their stories will only be remembered in eternity. While they are here they move on and give with His love with the same joy that they have received.

"Beloved, do not imitate what is evil, but what is good. He who does good is of God, but he who does evil has not seen God." (3 John 1:11 NKJV)

Duane

His name is Duane. When I first met him, I really didn't like him. I was very suspicious of his motives. Truthfully, I really didn't know him very well. As a youth pastor, I was pretty protective of our girls at church. I thought that he was some dude who was coming to our church just to meet our girls. You know the type. At least that's the way it seemed. Our youth group was filled with pretty teenage girls and his church didn't have any. He started visiting the youth service and I had my eye on him. I didn't trust this guy. I thought he was probably going to be bad news. I even called him something like "a Philistine."

Before long, his family had made the transition to our church and he was there to stay. He was a little older than the rest of the group and that meant he went off to college pretty quickly. Good - he's out of the picture, I thought. Well, several years later, he ended up marrying one of those young women and started a family. I guess he wasn't such a bad guy after all, but I still had my eye on him.

After I left the church as youth pastor, I became the District Youth Director in South Texas for all the Assemblies of God churches. It was a great honor and during that period of time, I would come back to the church, and I would see Duane and his wife Kayla. I would always hear good things about him, and he was working out to be a pretty good husband and provider. Sometimes when you have a hunch about someone, you're just dead wrong. Everything I thought about this guy ended up being the opposite. Don't judge too soon! I found out he was really a great guy. He worked hard and gave his best to whatever he attempted.

In 2001 when we came back to the church to pastor, one of our disappointments was there weren't a lot of young families. There were maybe three in the entire church. It was a very low demographic. The church was made up of older folks, and guess who was one of the young couples in the church? You got it, Duane and Kayla. That guy that I had my eye on and the guy I didn't trust. He and Kayla got married and had twin boys and then a little girl. They would be a beginning nucleus of many other young families coming to our church.

Later, when an opening came on the board, guess whose name went up for nomination? That's right – Duane, and he was voted in. Then in 2002 when I started talking about taking mission trips I still had him in my sights. I was watching him. I knew I needed to get him on a trip. I was dead wrong about this fellow. I could see he was a good man, and a good father, and he was a great husband. I could see he realized there was more to life than just getting up every day and going off to work, but that there's a God-appointed mission for every life. There's a purpose that God has for all of us. There's a purpose why God has put us here.

In 2003, I convinced him to go on a mission trip to Africa. I had to trick him, because he loves to hunt. I told him we would go on a safari at the end of the trip. I wasn't exactly sure how all that would work out, but our first trip was wonderful. We had wanted to go and build a church for a congregation who was worshiping under a tree. You read that right, a tree church. Many African congregations have nothing more than a local tree that they gather under. At least, that was what I had heard was needed, and that's what we were praying for. We were believing for the right tree church, in the right place, needing our team from Crossroads to build it.

One day I got a call from Jeff Gregory, our contact through Cornerstone Church in Nashville. He had found exactly that. Jeff was back in Kenya and he called just needing to tell me the good news. The Kenyan pastor who was his contact had gone with Jeff and the two of them had quite the story. Earlier that day they had found what we would later call The Tree Church. Jeff said that they had driven deep into the African bush and found this congregation needing a building. They were worshiping under a tree. He said, at first when they arrived they thought something was wrong. As they broke through the heavy foliage into a field, in their vehicle, they could see a group of women working the field using their machetes. When they saw the land cruiser, these women started running toward them and yelling at the top of their lungs waving these long knives. Jeff and the pastor were startled and at first thought "This is not good! We are being attacked! What have we done wrong?" But something powerful was in the works.

That morning the pastor's wife had said the Lord had spoken to her and said, "You need to clear the property for the new church. They are coming to build your new building." So, they had gone to this field and were hacking away with their hoes, machetes and picks. Here's the big 30,000-foot picture of this event. This is the African bush. There are no phones near these people. This is in the early 2000s. Even cell phones were not as frequent out in this part of the world as they are today. There is no way they had any knowledge by any means other than the Holy Spirit that this was about to happen. As Jeff and his Kenyan national pastor got out of the vehicle they realized the ladies were celebrating. They knew that when they saw the vehicle arriving that yes God had heard their prayers and the people who were coming to build their building had arrived. When Jeff heard what the pastor's wife had said, he began to cry as he realized God was all over this project, and Crossroads had found their church to build. When he called me and told me the story I remember I was on a mission tour for Speed the Light in Arkansas. I cried too. I thought how great and how big our God is that He can speak to a pastor in Texas about a church needing to be built, somewhere in Africa, and a man from Tennessee is the messenger, and a pastor's wife in Kenya can tell everyone to get ready because they're coming. And at the exact time that the messenger from Tennessee arrives with the good news, they just happen to be clearing the property for the church. That's living in the overflow. That's the power of the Holy Spirit. He still works in people's lives today. That's allowing His voice to speak and quiet the fears and doubts and let faith speak when it seems it's impossible for this to ever happen.

So, we traveled to Kenya and Duane was never the same. God had put him on my heart and I wanted to make sure he made that trip. He told me later, "I really did want to go on the trip, but it was mainly for the animals, but then I saw what a difference we could make in the lives of the people. This was for me!" I remember watching it move Duane and Kayla in a big way.

Now these church buildings are not like your elaborate crystal cathedrals or even pretty little country churches. No sir. These African buildings are basically your pole barn. A simple structure of steel girders and rafters and purlins with a tin roof. No walls - just a roof. Because that's the main thing. They need to get out of the rain and the heat of the day. The shade of the roof and the protection from the seasonal downpours is the main thing.

I'll never forget that first trip. Every time I looked up during that trip, I saw Duane working. He was digging footings and he was up on that roof, running a screw gun. He was there at the beginning of the day until the end. He became like a foreman with Jeff. He absorbed every part of the construction of one of these buildings. He was hooked! I was hooked too!

On a side note, my wife Danielle was on that trip and got to help the national ladies prepare our lunches. I had been on many overseas trips and had the opportunity to eat many different meals: cobra, dog, monkey, ox, and a mountain of chicken, but one day they brought one of the goats as the main guest. This precious little city girl got to help in the whole process making that goat our lunch. What an adventure that was for her and for our team to be eating out on the African plains while building a church. It was absolutely wonderful. I cry as I write this, not realizing at the time how wonderful that very first trip was. Every day we drove out there and for those three days or so that it took to put up that first church we were awestruck at this new passion. These disciples were really taking the Gospel to the ends of the earth. I would step back and watch, and my heart would just about burst through my chest as I thought of how different our church was becoming. This was what I had dreamed of.

Duane and New Masaai Friends

On the last day, there was a celebration. The pastor said that we would gather at the old tree church and then we would have a parade to the new church building. Back home we were talking of buying land and building our own new church building. We had had some meetings and a piece of property had come available. We were believing some miracle would take place that we might be able to build this grand dream. For us it was just about as impossible as it was for this little African congregation to have what they were now possessing. Their building was around $5,000 dollars. Our new building was around $5 million dollars. Yeah, pretty close to the same miracle in size. There was no way they would ever have that much money and I don't know what we were thinking... we still had to buy the land for $2.5 million.

As we all made our way to the tree church there was excitement. I could see Jeff getting ready to speak and Duane wasn't far away. We sang some wonderful Masaai worship songs and the people danced and shouted.

Before I knew it, we were all dancing. We were celebrating the overflow of God's blessings on this little church in Africa. Then the parade began. About a hundred yards or so to the new building we began to dance. With heads rocking back and forth as only the Masaai can do, we danced in a walk-like-manner, all the way to that new building. Shouting, singing, celebrating, and excitement was on everyone's face. People were wiping their faces with their aprons and shirt sleeves as the tears coursed down their cheeks. It was a wonderful commotion of praise and worship.

"Because you've done this for us..."

At some point the pastor's wife, who had told everyone months before that we were coming, began to prophesy again. She said, *"Because you have done this for us, the Lord will do this for you!"* I'll never forget that. As long as I live I'll never forget that moment. When we were in the big middle of our disaster trying to complete the Crossroads building, and the meltdown of 2008, I had a picture of that church dedication on my wall. It was hanging in the job site trailer, out by the funeral home we were using for offices, and our Wednesday night sanctuary. We all stood out by that metal pole barn that became a church and took that now famous picture. It was a great team of folks from Crossroads. Mixed in the group was the congregation of the tree church. It was like one big church. We were together in this. Partners in the harvest. It's been around 15 years since that first trip and we've built many more buildings. In fact, Duane went back and helped build nine more churches. Some of those trips I was on and some Duane led by himself. He was really becoming a real gift to me, and to Crossroads. Beware pastors: the punk kid scoping out your girls in your youth group might one day become a great friend and deacon. I remember that trip really having an effect on Duane and Kayla. When we ended the mission part of the trip and went on the safari. I saw Duane and Kayla having several deep prayerful conversations. The mission part of the trip had moved them in a powerful way. They would never be the same. God's hand has been on them ever since.

The Tree Church tabernacle completed

Before I knew it, we heard of a mission work in Haiti. It was a school and villages of hurting people. Mountain people needing the hugs and love and prayer that Crossroads needed to give. Acts 29 and its leader Don Adamson have been a great partner for Crossroads in Haiti. Duane has led trip after trip to that spiritually broken island nation. He's carried untold amounts of food, toys and supplies to the mountains and helped disciple other people in the joy of serving in missions.

I'm really proud to be his pastor. He's one man that I have the greatest respect for and confidence in. It's great to find leaders who will get in the overflow with you. That's exactly what Duane has done. He first got in the flow and now He's gotten in the overflow. He's out in the middle of it. He's helping reach others for Christ. He's a gentle, loving leader who takes time to show others the joy of the overflow. If you ever get a chance to go on a mission trip with Duane, you'll love it. If you are a pastor's friend, and don't mind working, maybe the Lord could use you like he's used Duane.

The one thing I've always loved about Duane is that he's always given me honor as pastor. He's never tried to override one of my decisions. I celebrate the goodness of this man. He is a Barnabas-type leader. The Bible said about Barnabas:

"For he was a good man, full of the Holy Spirit and of faith." *(Acts 11:24a NKJV)*

That's a perfect description of Duane. When you see God using someone like he's used Duane, you can't help but respect them. He's the real deal. Truly he has never crossed one of my decisions. He has never held back an opinion, but he has always honored me as the final authority on any topic. He's been a genuine gift to me as a pastor. Very loving and caring. A true armor bearer. When I was facing some of the darkest days as pastor of this church he stood right there with me. I will always love and respect him for that.

God has blessed me with a truly great team. One old African tribesman we met a few years ago was named Joseph. He was in his late eighties when we met him one night out by a campfire. He had an old Maasai sword hanging from a tattered belt-like-strap. He was telling us stories about the old Kenya, and what it was like to be raised in the African bush. I asked him if he had ever killed a lion with that sword? He said, "You know, you can't kill a lion alone. It takes a team of people." I said, "What do you mean?" He told me that when they would hunt a lion that it would take twenty or so of the Maasai warriors to join together. They would circle the lion and taunt him and finally they would wear him down and attack him. He said, "You can't attack a lion alone!" I'll never forget that. It takes a team to kill a lion. Thank you Lord for the team you've given me. I am a blessed pastor. All of our board of advisors, pastors and staff members are amazing. I love them so much and believe for heaven's best over them.

"(*Do Good to Please God*) "Take heed that you do not do your charitable deeds before men, to be seen by them. Otherwise you have no reward from your Father in heaven." (Matthew 6:1 NKJV)

Duane has never been one to sound his horn or make a big deal about all God has helped him to do. But I want to give a little honor to whom honor is due. Duane will never tell you that there's a village in the mountains of Haiti that's known as

Duaneville. It's named after him. He went there so much and loved those people so much they decided they would just call It Duaneville. He would never tell you about the kids he and Kayla sponsor through One Child. It is an organization that feeds tens of thousands of children every day and helps in developing their futures in Christ. He might if he thought you would sponsor a child yourself, but not to brag on himself. A very humble and genuine follower of Christ, that's Duane Cannon.

On the day of this picture, everyone in
Duaneville had just received Christ as their Savior!

Duaneville

Several years ago, Duane started a project in Haiti to bring Christmas to all the kids and families. Right before December 25, for the last half-dozen years or so, he has led the charge to take about 1,500-2,000 toys to the kids there in Ropissa and to distribute elder kits of rice, beans, oil, and flour for the widows and elders of the mountains. His family has taken their vacations to go on mission trips year after year. They have influenced nations for Christ. I weep while I write this. That's living in the overflow. But Duane would never tell you this. If you ever heard it, it would be to encourage you to join him and just what it might do to help you see how much Christ loves the people there, but nothing about him. God give me some more Duane Cannons!

"I am the vine, you *are* the branches. He who abides in Me, and I in him, bears much fruit; for without Me you can do nothing. ⁶ If anyone does not abide in Me, he is cast out as a branch and is withered; and they gather them and throw *them* into the fire, and they are burned. ⁷ If you abide in Me, and My words abide in you, you will ask what you desire, and it shall be done for you. ⁸ By this My Father is glorified, that you bear much fruit; so, you will be My disciples." (John 15:5-8 NKJV)

"Every tree that does not bear good fruit is cut down and thrown into the fire." (Matthew 7:19 NKJV)

So many Christians today are fruitless trees. They are barren from any good works. Christ's love has been kept hidden in their hearts. Like a treasure that they wouldn't ever take out and give away. He is locked in their heart like a diamond of great value only to be horded and loved by its owner, but never to be shared. Duane is a rare find. He shows up many mornings for early prayer and spends a little time drinking coffee with his pastor. He's a gift, a friend, a confidant and he lives in the overflow.

This past summer we were leaving for another African trip, but this time we were headed to two countries: Tanzania and Kenya. This was a first for us. Seeing our kids in Kenya and then heading to Tanzania to build onto a school there. It was a big undertaking and very taxing, but it was worth it. Living in the overflow sometimes will cost you energy, finances, and time but it will be worth it. The changed lives are all that matters.

Duane Bringing Christmas to Haiti

On the eve of leaving for this trip Duane's work bag is stolen out of his truck. In that bag are two laptops. These are work computers. Duane is a building contractor and he primarily builds churches. This was a terrible thing to have happen on the way out of the country. So many files on those computers and the communication back with his office while he was away and not having a computer. This was a bad situation. At first, he said he thought about getting upset and mad about it but then he said, "I thought, I'll just pray for the guy. I'll give the devil a black eye on this."

"But I say to you, love your enemies, bless those who curse you, do good to those who hate you, and pray for those who spitefully use you and persecute you," (Matthew 5:44 NKJV)

Fortunately, there was a guy who saw Duane's truck get broken into and he tried to follow the thief who stole Duane's bag with the two laptops. The man came back and told Duane he almost caught up to the guy. Duane told him that his bag had been stolen and that he appreciated him trying to help. He explained he was leaving in a day or so for Africa on a mission trip. He shared a little bit about what the trip was about and immediately the guy said, "Man I've wanted to do something like that! One day I want to go on mission trip!" Little did he know, he was speaking to the right guy. At that moment God began to turn this terrible situation into a God moment. Of course, it was hard at the time to get into all that was involved in the trip we were taking but Duane spent a little time there ministering to this man about missions and what God was doing through our church and what he might consider doing in the future. He took his cell number and told him I'll call when we get back. When you live on mission and you live in the overflow there is something about how God will put events together. He will turn the junk the devil does into a great thing.

"But as for you, you meant evil against me; *but* God meant it for good, in order to bring it about as *it is* this day, to save many people alive." (Genesis 50:20 NKJV)

A few months later that lunch took place. It just so happened Don Adamson, the missionary over Acts 29, was in town and joined Duane for the lunch. This guy was in for a treat. Don and Duane began to tell him all about what God was doing in Haiti. To hear Duane tell the story, the man was trying to interrupt him while they were talking. Duane was explaining about the school there in Haiti. He told him that we had our first trip where teachers and educators were going to help with the school, this past spring. All the while Duane and Don are talking this guy is trying to interrupt them. He said, *"Wait a minute - I have to say this. My business partner and I, we take and refurbish schools. We have a lot of equipment you might could use."*

Here's Just How Amazing God is

The man with the equipment had 42 laptops and the charging towers that he wanted to give to the school in Haiti. At the time of this writing there is more. A possible huge generator, water pumps to irrigate farms in Haiti and more.

"But whoever has this world's goods, and sees his brother in need, and shuts up his heart from him, how does the love of God abide in him?" (1 John 3:17 NKJV)

God turned around a loss of two laptops and gave back 42 laptops and a tower charging station. A school in Haiti is receiving that overflow. I like that kind of overflow. It's all a part of the overflow from a once-punk kid who I didn't like coming to our youth group. His first intentions might have been wrong, but God knows how to grab our hearts. Who knew what he would end up becoming? I would have never dreamed that guy would have become who he is today. Who would have dreamed he would lead an annual Christmas push for kids in Haiti so that 2,000 kids could get something for Christmas? Who would have believed that he would be the guy with the dream, to bless elders and widows of those mountain communities with essentials, and gifts for their Christmas?

"Then the righteous will answer Him, saying, 'Lord, when did we see You hungry and feed *You,* or thirsty and give *You drink?* [38] When did we see You a stranger and take *You* in, or naked and clothe *You?* [39] Or when did we see You sick, or in prison, and come to You?' [40] And the King will answer and say to them, 'Assuredly, I say to you, inasmuch as you did *it* to one of the least of these My brethren, you did *it* to Me.' (Matthew 25:37-40 NKJV)

Duane tying a little Haitian girl's shoes

"Your true character is most accurately measured by how you treat those who can do nothing for you."
Mother Teresa

Let it Flow!

Study Guide Questions for Chapter 11
Create a Tsunami of Love!
Every Action Has a Reaction!

Matthew 25:21 NKJV
"His lord said to him, 'Well *done,* good and faithful servant; you were faithful over a few things, I will make you ruler over many things. Enter into the joy of your lord.'"

E very action has an equal and opposite reaction. Newton's law of motion explains that physical law has a relationship with all mechanical actions. In essence all energy of force and motion will have an equal and reverse energy of force and motion. The same can be said for actions of love and giving. When I give and let love overflow from my life it can have a huge impact on the life of someone else. It's like watching dominoes fall. One triggers a line and before you know it, they are all falling over because of the effect of one. One domino moves the rest. That's how the momentum of love affects others.

What Have You Been Called to Be Faithful Over?

_____

_____

_____

3 John 1:11 NKJV
"Beloved, do not imitate what is evil, but what is good. He who does good is of God, but he who does evil has not seen God."

Besides Christ Who Would You Like to Be Like?

_____

_____

How Could You Be a Greater Blessing to Others than You've Been?

_____
_____
_____
_____

–

Matthew 6:1 NKJV

"(*Do Good to Please God*) "Take heed that you do not do your charitable deeds before men, to be seen by them. Otherwise you have no reward from your Father in heaven."

Matthew 7:19 NKJV

"Every tree that does not bear good fruit is cut down and thrown into the fire."

What Tsunami or Wave of Love Would You Like to See Christ Create Around You?

_____
_____
_____
_____

Genesis 50:20 NKJV

"But as for you, you meant evil against me; *but* God meant it for good, in order to bring it about as *it is* this day, to save many people alive."

Comments

_____
_____
_____
_____

A natural cross I found at the bottom of a tree
at one of our tree churches we built a tabernacle for in Africa.
To some it might look like a stick; to me it looked like
this little cross was praising the Lord!
"Let everything that hath breath praise the Lord" Psalm 150:6a

In Closing:

As I come to the conclusion of this book there are so many more wonderful people that I could and probably will write about. People who have lived in the overflow of God's love. Who have poured their hearts and lives out onto others. Perhaps in the future I will write about more people living in the overflow.

I have truly enjoyed the times of reflection and of getting away and diving back into these stories. Every one of these amazing, wonderful people are to be celebrated. I hope I have added some value to each of them and to the cause of Christ.

Like the killing of a lion it takes a team to write a book. One of those people is Kenneth Hall. What a great day it was when I met you. You have been a huge blessing to me and my ministry. Let me say a big thank-you to Kenneth, my editor for all the countless hours you spent poring over this manuscript and for developing the grammatical structure of this book in a readable form. Thank you for all your help you've given to this poorly educated preacher. You are my hero!

To the people whose stories I've shared in this book - thank you. Your life has been an inspiration to me, and to others. You have blessed me as I've watched you grow in living in the overflow. Your sacrifice and love for others is a story that must be repeated over and over. I pray you never lose your fervency to give, care and love.

To my wife Danielle, thank you for putting up with me for these past forty years. Thank you for living your life in the overflow. I've never seen a more dedicated mother, nana and wife than you. You inspire me to try harder and be a better man in every way. The Lord willing, I pray we can enjoy another forty years of marriage together. What a blessed woman you are to get a guy like me (wink).

To my wonderful children, you are the best. Mom and I started this family at a pretty young age. She was way ahead of the curve on what a great parent was supposed to be. I lacked a lot of skills in the parenting department. Thank you for being patient with me as I have tried to get better at being a dad. Each of you possesses a beautiful gift of living life to the best and fullest. You are a gift to me. I love you dearly. My greatest desire is to see you all make heaven. I draw strength from each of you, and you make me so proud. Thank you for being who you are and for always being there for me.

To those of you who have encouraged me to continue to write after I completed Never Give Up. That was a journey of digging into the hardest, most difficult places of my life. That was a time of great trial and I was raw in emotion as I peeled back the layers of hurt. Thank you.

This book has been a completely different journey. I've reflected over and over on the amazing, wonderful things God has done in my life. I have reminisced on some of the heroes I've encountered and victories I've seen God accomplish, and people I've met. There are so many more people whose name I should list, but I would surely fail to mention someone. At the risk of missing someone let me just say thank you to all of you. Thank you for encouraging, loving and lifting me up every day. I feel so blessed.

To my board of advisors, pastoral team, staff, and congergation of Crossroads Fellowship you truly are a joy to my life. I'm so glad back in 1982 Danielle and I were invited to come to Houston and be a part of this church. Little did we know how much that phone call would change our lives forever. Who knew the kids who were leading youth, children and providing some janitorial services would end up where we landed? Things have really worked out so well for us. We are forever grateful for your love, kindness and generosity. Your hearts have blessed us beyond anything we could imagine. We have lived in the overflow of your love.

The overflow is something we all can be a part of. We can choose to live this life in the overflow for Christ, or we can allow our life to overflow in something else. The overflow is finding your life's mission. It's discovering the theme of your life and living that theme and mission out. What a privilege when you find that the overflow is living life with Christ.

The stories are many. Definitely too many to put into just one book. From the divorced single mom of two boys thinking that life was over. Her what's-the-use story, to the finding life and building futures story in helping other hurting boys and girls at Christmas, to the punk kid who becomes a wonderful leader in our church. All of these are stories of the overflow. People who have learned the joy of loving and serving others. They've experienced the deep, refreshing waters of God's generosity and want to splash it on everyone they can find. It's creating that tidal wave of caring and being the overflow. I hope you enjoy reading Living in the Overflow and that you will create your own tsunami of love.

"My Heart is Overflowing…"
Psalm 45:1a NKJV

About the Author

Reverend Mike Allard began preaching as a boy when he was just thirteen years old in his home church, Northwest Assembly of God in Wichita Falls, Texas. He received his first preaching credential, The Christian Worker's Permit, March 9, 1976, at the age of fifteen. He as wlicensed at nineteen and has been ordained for the past thirty-three years.

During his years of ministry, he has served as youth pastor and children's pastor for eleven years; as District Youth Director in South Texas for eleven years and the Lead Pastor at Crossroads Fellowship, in Houston, Texas for the past eighteen years.

He was elected to the South Texas District Assemblies of God Presbytery as an Executive Presbyter in 2016.

He is the author of the book: "Never Give Up!" It is the incredible true story of how God brought him from failure to faith.

Crossroads Fellowship, under the leadership of Pastor Mike has grown from 250 to an average of 1,500 each Sunday.

Pastor Mike has a passion for souls and missions. In his many years of travel, he has raised millions of dollars in mission services, conferences, conventions, camps, tours, and on special days. Over the past three years, Crossroads Fellowship has given each year over $1,000,000 to missions.

But his greatest accomplishment is his family. He has a beautiful wife Danielle who has been by his side for 40 years. He has three wonderful children, Joshua, Michael and Lacey. He has ten grandchildren, and he looks forward to every day getting to share life with this crazy, wonderful family God has given him.

Another Book by Mike Allard

You can access this book through **Kindle** Unlimited or pay $7.99 to buy on Kindle.

Paperback copies $9.99 through Amazon.com

You can **receive a FREE copy** of Never Give Up when you attend one of Crossroads Fellowship's weekend services as a first-time

Never Give Up!
Lessons the Lord Taught Me When I Wanted to Quit!

What's Inside of Never Give Up?

For years, Pastor Mike Allard has told the congregation of Crossroads Fellowship in Houston, Texas, that "We shouldn't have made it." This book is the true story of his journey from failure to faith. It's the story of how the church overcame some tremendous obstacles - how the Lord turned a disastrous situation around. Its pages chronicle Pastor Mike's descent into a deep valley of depression as the Great Recession hit his church head-on in the middle of a massive building program!

With millions of dollars owed and nowhere to turn, Pastor Mike turned to the one, and only one, who could change his destiny. His recovery wasn't easy. The man with a Midas touch, who had encountered success after success, found himself mired in the greatest failure of his life. This book is a great book for encouraging someone who has gone through or is going through a difficult trial that has no end in sight. It reminds us that the Lord is always there. It is for the person who's living in a dark place and who needs to know that the God of the impossible is still a miracle-working Savior. Nothing is impossible for our God! You will be riveted and touched by Pastor Mike's refreshing and disarming honesty and frankness as he opens doors to private rooms in his emotional house. You will enjoy the story as it unfolds, and you will rejoice as God's sovereign hand moves and changes Pastor Mike's story.

For Testimonials

...of how you have been affected by the book Never Give Up and its effect on your life please send an email directly to Pastor Mike at: mikeallard@mac.com

Crossroads Fellowship
713-455-1661
12110 E Sam Houston Pkwy N
Houston, Texas 77044

Large Orders of "Never Give Up!" or "Living in the Overflow!"

Special Pricing is available for quantities over 25 copies. Please feel free to contact Pastor Mike through the above email!

Made in the USA
Lexington, KY
14 December 2019

58514713R00133